Yoga and Cardiovascular Management

Yoga and Cardiovascular Management

Discussions with

Swami Satyananda Saraswati

Research correlated by

Dr Swami Karmananda Saraswati MBBS (Syd)

Yoga Publications Trust, Munger, Bihar, India

Printed by Bihar School of Yoga
    First published 1982
    Second edition 1984

Printed by Yoga Publications Trust
    Reprinted 2001

ISBN: 81-85787-26-3
Indian edition: Rupees

Publisher and distributor: Yoga Publications Trust, Ganga Darshan, Munger, Bihar, India.

Website: www.yogavision.net
E-mail: ypt@yogavision.net

Printed at Thomson Press (India) Limited, New Delhi, 110001

SWAMI SIVANANDA SARASWATI

Swami Sivananda was born at Patta-madai, Tamil Nadu, in 1887. After serving as a medical doctor in Malaya, he renounced his practice, went to Rishikesh and was initiated into Dash-nami sannyasa in 1924 by Swami Vishwananda Saraswati. He toured extensively throughout India, inspiring people to practise yoga and lead a divine life. He founded the Divine Life Society at Rishikesh in 1936, the Sivananda Ayurvedic Pharmacy in 1945, the Yoga Vedanta Forest Academy in 1948 and the Sivananda Eye Hospital in 1957. During his lifetime Swami Sivananda guided thousands of disciples and aspirants all over the world and authored over 200 books.

SWAMI SATYANANDA SARASWATI

Swami Satyananda was born at Almora, Uttar Pradesh, in 1923. In 1943 he met Swami Sivananda in Rishikesh and adopted the Dashnami sannyasa way of life. In 1955 he left his guru's ashram to live as a wandering mendicant and later founded the International Yoga Fellowship in 1963 and the Bihar School of Yoga in 1964. Over the next 20 years Swami Satyananda toured internation-ally and authored over 80 books. In 1987 he founded Sivananda Math, a charitable institution for aiding rural development, and the Yoga Research Foundation. In 1988 he renounced his mission, adopting kshetra sannyasa, and now lives as a paramahamsa sannyasin.

SWAMI NIRANJANANANDA SARASWATI

Swami Niranjanananda was born at Rajnandgaon, Madhya Pradesh, in 1960. At the age of four he joined the Bihar School of Yoga and was initiated into Dashnami sannyasa at the age of ten. From 1971 he travelled overseas and toured many countries for the next 11 years. In 1983 he was recalled to India and appointed President of Bihar School of Yoga. During the following 11 years he guided the development of Ganga Darshan, Sivananda Math and the Yoga Research Foundation. In 1990 he was initiated as a paramahamsa and in 1993 anointed preceptor in succession to Swami Satyananda. Bihar Yoga Bharati was founded under his direction in 1994. He has authored over 20 books and guides national and international yoga programs.

SWAMI SATYASANGANANDA SARASWATI

Swami Satyasangananda (Satsangi) was born on 24th March 1953, in Chandorenagore, West Bengal. From the age of 22 she experienced a series of inner awakenings which led her to her guru, Swami Satyananda. From 1981 she travelled ceaselessly with her guru in India and overseas and developed into a scholar with deep insight into the yogic and tantric traditions as well as modern sciences and philosophies. She is an efficient channel for the transmission of her guru's teachings. The establishment of Sivananda Math in Rikhia is her creation and mission, and she guides all its activities there, working tirelessly to uplift the weaker and underprivileged areas. She embodies compassion with clear reason and is the foundation of her guru's vision.

Contents

Preface

This is a unique record of the discussions between Swami Satyananda Saraswati and the group of French medical experts, physicians, yoga teachers and journalists who gathered to participate in and share their views on 'Yoga and Medical Management of Cardiovascular Disease' at Tenon Hospital, Paris, on 16 September 1981.

The discussions were led by Professor Cloarec, one of Europe's leading pathologists, and Dr Christiane Daussy, head of the Yoga and Relaxation Department at the hospital. Professor Cloarec's prime research has been the stress-related diseases of civilization, and he has pioneered the recognition and adaptation of yoga in the clinical management of cardiovascular diseases.

This meeting marked a decisive and historic turning point in the relationship between medicine and yoga. Throughout the discussions, there was active collaboration between the two sciences. The technological attainments of modern medicine were integrated with the yogic understanding of human psychophysiology. The outcome promises to be a more complete, humane and enlightened therapeutic science in the years ahead.

Introduction to Heart Disease

Heart disease is by far the number one killer in the technological and industrialized societies of today. Its rising incidence has been truly phenomenal. Consider these statistics: in 1905, 25% of all deaths in the USA were due to coronary heart disease or its complications; by 1955 the figure had risen to 55%, and today 70% of all deaths occurring in the USA are due to cardiovascular disease. In 1969 the Executive Board of the World Health Organization (WHO) described heart disease as 'the greatest epidemic mankind has faced'.

Even in India, heart disease has become the third largest killer amongst the city dwellers who adhere to the modern lifestyle, but fortunately, it remains a rarity in the villages, where 85% of the population lives, following a simple, natural and stress-free lifestyle.

More encouraging statistics came to light in a study conducted by the University of Texas Health Science Centre[1], which recorded that there was actually a dramatic decrease in deaths from heart disease in America between 1968 and 1976.

The death rate from coronary disease decreased by 20.7% during that period, and I am sure the same trend is being recorded in other countries as well. The researchers concluded that this promising trend can be attributed to two major factors:

1

1. Changes in lifestyle, including a more natural diet containing less animal fats and cholesterol, decrease in cigarette smoking, etc.
2. Improved medical care, especially in the acute coronary cases.

To these two factors I would venture to add a third one. There has definitely been an awakening of spiritual awareness on our planet in the last decade, and in this, yoga has been at the forefront. The impact of yoga upon a culture is as subtle as it is profound. A gradual transformation of consciousness is occurring. People everywhere are more health conscious, more diet conscious and more conscious of yoga. Whether they practise or not, definitely a very high proportion of people today are now aware of yoga asanas, relaxation, meditation, dietary and living habits, and the physical and mental benefits they bestow. Almost everyone is making some effort to improve in a practical, spiritual way. Even if they are not, they definitely want to. This is yoga and this is also preventive medicine. Yoga has an enormous role to play in the preventive medicine of the future. By preventive medicine I mean what we can do now by way of personal and social actions to ensure that our family members and friends do not suffer and die prematurely as so many do today, facing heart attacks even in the fourth or fifth decade of life.

The remarkable achievements of modern medical science in managing acute heart disease must be acknowledged. Nevertheless, as doctors, you yourselves have sought to incorporate yoga into this sphere of medical management, and most of our questions reflect this. They concern management or cure of major cardiac conditions using yoga. Yoga definitely has a role to play here, and I will do my best to indicate specific yoga techniques which will be useful in your own practices, as you have asked.

Nevertheless, do not forget that yoga primarily concerns health and not disease; it is a spiritual science, not a material one. Spirit always remains healthy while matter, of its very nature, is subject to decay and death. This body is born, so it must die. It is inevitable. Modern medical science focuses its attention upon the individual manifested forms of the material creation, and as such it is a study of pathology in itself. So, yoga has much to offer and medical science has much to gain.

Question 1

Yogic Pathology

Have you explored a pathological field?
This is a difficult philosophical question because the extent to which physiology (normal function) and pathology (disease) overlap is really a matter of personal experience. Just as all the dualities of life – pleasure and pain, love and hate, joy and sorrow, attachment and aversion, life and death are really two sides of one coin, so physiology and pathology are really only two different ways of viewing the phenomenon of life in a human body. There is no physiology without pathology, nor can there be pathology without physiology.

I believe that human life is an interaction of pathological and physiological forces. These same twin and opposed forces have been conceptualized as good and evil in the religious systems of the past. In religion and also in medicine, the twin forces are imagined to be in opposition to one another. One is good, healthy and to be sought after; the other is bad, diseased and to be rejected. This duality of thought, this split in consciousness, is the only real pathology in creation. Without this schizophrenic break, all life is one and continuous.

In tantra, the twin forces are also recognized. They are known as shiva and shakti, ida and pingala, purusha and prakriti. However, we do not recognize that one is good and one is bad. In India there are tantric cults dedicated to both principles. Some worship the imperishable conscious-ness (shiva, health), others worship the ever-changing manifesting matter (shakti, disease). Both are necessary in human evolution, and both are ways to transcend the duality of vision which is our only real pathology. After all, how can there be pleasure without pain, how can there be life without death, how can there be health without disease? It is unfeasible and impractical. Therefore, in tantra we realize that shiva and shakti are in cooperation; they are working together in order to relentlessly evolve conscious-ness from the clutches of matter.

According to tantra and yoga, it is not life or death which is to be sought, nor pleasure or pain. Rather, the purpose of living and dying is to experience and to evolve the awareness. This experience and this path of evolving and transcending the awareness beyond the confines of duality is known as yoga. Yoga is the vision of union between physiology and pathology, life and death, pleasure and pain; it leads to sublime equanimity, bliss and eternal life.

To the extent that I have lived life, I have definitely been exploring a pathological field, but at the same time I have managed to maintain an awareness of the spectrum of life as a physiological unfoldment also. Is human birth physiological or pathological? According to some spiritual philosophies, human birth is the pathology; the body of bones, blood and bile is the only disease and life within it is a valley of pain and suffering. For others, liberation lies beyond death in heaven. For a materialist, death is pain and destruction for eternity. But I do not accept any of these ideals or philosophies. For me, life itself is all fullness, and whatever it brings me is satisfactory and sufficient. I do not differentiate; I accept all. And what about death? It is just a part of life, that is all.

Hypertension

At present, anti-hypertensive drugs leave much to be desired. Can yoga offer an alternative treatment?
Hypertension refers to a consistently elevated blood pressure level. Blood pressure is recorded as two readings, namely, SBP/DBP (systolic blood pressure/diastolic blood pressure). Transient elevations of systolic blood pressure occur in normal people under conditions such as exercise and emotional states such as anger. However, a consistently elevated diastolic blood pressure, which reflects the baseline pressure level in the arterial network, is considered most significant in diagnosis and assessment of the severity of hypertension. The point when treatment of blood pressure should begin and a patient should be labelled hypertensive is by no means clear-cut. It is hotly debated in medical circles. As a general guideline, the upper limit of normal is considered to be (100+age)/90, but it varies from doctor to doctor, country to country and year to year.

In general, a diastolic blood pressure above 90 is today considered to warrant institution of lifelong anti-hypertensive drug therapy, even though the patient usually remains free of any symptoms.

The doctor's dilemma

Why try to control a high blood pressure which remains symptomless? This is the basic dilemma faced by doctors

6

today and it also points to the widespread use of yoga nidra as the first line of medical treatment for mild to moderate hypertension in the future.

The effects of a continuing uncontrolled elevation of blood pressure over months or years are found to be harmful, and in some cases even disastrous. Degeneration of blood vessels (arteriosclerosis), predisposing to death by cerebral stroke; kidney damage leading to progressive electrolyte disturbance, auto-intoxication and renal failure; and damage to the heart leading to gradually progressive heart failure and predisposing to acute myocardial infarction, are only a few of the more severe long-term effects.

Cardiovascular mortality constitutes up to 50% of the total mortality in our technologically advanced communities and hypertension is one of the most common cardiovascular disease processes. Clearly, some form of therapy is demanded to lower the blood pressure to satisfactory levels to prevent future complications and early death.

In spite of this knowledge, only 50% of hypertensives are presently detected, and only about 25% are adequately controlled on anti-hypertensive therapy. A very high proportion of patients drop out of treatment, or fail to comply with it closely. The reasons for this are simple:

• Only at high levels of blood pressure are troublesome symptoms produced, such as dizziness, pounding headache, ringing in the ears, nausea and tiredness. In its beginning stages, hypertension is an asymptomatic disease. Sufferers do not feel sick, although their blood vessels and organs are relentlessly degenerating at an accelerated rate, unknown to them.

• Anti-hypertensive drugs are powerful and potentially dangerous. There are many types of drugs and they must be combined in various regimes or combinations. No uniform opinion as to the best regime exists and frequent readjustment, reassessment and follow-up is required. This demands a cooperative and willing patient. Yet it is difficult to persuade patients to accept

7

such drug therapy when their disease causes them no symptoms and the therapy subjects them to unpleasant side effects for the rest of their lives. This is without mentioning the major dangers of many of the drugs, some of which have been related with increased risk of cancers, etc. Many patients feel the cure is worse than the disease, thus the high dropout rate from treatment.

The anti-hypertensive drugs

Some of the drug groups used in anti-hypertensive therapy are given below. Their effects and side effects are also indicated.

- *Diuretics*: act upon the kidneys, promoting urine production to decrease body fluids and blood pressure. Side effects are reflex hypotension, electrolyte depletion, cardiac arrhythmia.
- *B-blockers*: slow the heart rate by blocking sympathetic (excitatory) nervous influences upon the heart. Nightmares and other side effects have been reported.
- *Methyl dopa*: slows the heart. Side effects are drowsiness, sexual disturbances in males, depression and sleep disturbances.
- *Peripheral vasodilators*: cause a dilation of peripheral blood vessels and capillary beds. Side effects are severe hypotension, fainting, etc.
- *Calcium channel blockers*: which reduce an excitatory effect of calcium ions on the smooth muscles of blood vessels and on the heart muscle itself, ensuring variable and dose-dependent vasodilation of coronary arteries and reduced contractibility of heart muscle.
- *Centrally acting drugs*: sedatives, hypnotics and tranquillizers which act upon the hypothalamus and other brain centres to counteract central tension and stress levels. Side effects are altered moods, impaired mental functioning, nervous symptoms, tiredness, etc.

Many doctors have always questioned the value of seeking to institute anti-hypertensive therapy. Is it really

8

feasible to institute drug therapy which is costly, demands careful monitoring and frequent adjustment, and produces dangerous or troublesome side effects for such a high proportion of the population and for the remainder of their lives? In the past there was no alternative, but in recent years, yoga nidra has been shown to be an economical and effective adjunct in hypertension management, and it seems to be only a matter of time before it emerges as a major weapon in the prevention and management of mild to moderate hypertension.

Classification of basic types of hypertension

The cause of 90% of hypertension cases remains unknown to modern medical science. This is termed idiopathic or essential hypertension. At present, the only form of treatment available is anti-hypertensive drugs, which leave so much to be desired.

The remaining 10% of cases of hypertension occur secondary to some recognizable physical cause, such as diseases of the kidneys, aorta or endocrine glands (e.g. adrenal gland tumour) for which some specific form of medical or surgical therapy often proves curative.

Aetiology of essential hypertension

In spite of the material security of modern life, man is nevertheless subjected to a far greater continuing burden of stress today than at any time in his long history. In the past, his physical existence, comfort and security may have been intermittently threatened by wars and natural catastrophes, but now his intrapsychic and emotional realms are in a constant state of siege and know no peace whatsoever. Technological and economic advancement has created a way of life in which the individual cannot keep pace. Mental stress and strain are the penalties we pay for becoming 'civilized'. In this sense, hypertension is an 'evolutionary' disease, whose increasing incidence has closely paralleled the rise in stress levels in modern times.

9

No one is immune to stress, but the threshold varies from individual to individual. One of the most important roles of yoga for the modern individual is to increase the psychological and physiological capacities to resist stress. Stress affects different parts of the body and can lead to various diseases, according to the psychic and physical peculiarities of each individual, such as body type, emotional make-up, hereditary influences, etc.

Intrapsychic and environmental stress is clearly implicated as a cause of essential hypertension. Urban populations have been shown to have higher blood pressure levels than village dwellers, for whom stress intrudes much less into the daily routine.[1] Higher standards of living, better education, higher incomes and more skilled occupations are all associated with elevated blood pressure. Some jobs have been shown to be more stressful than others. Executives, professionals and people working in jobs with deadlines are under greater stress, and these professions are predisposed to coronary disease and hypertension.[2]

Factors of diet, heredity, obesity, smoking and lack of exercise have also been implicated but appear to play secondary roles.[3]

Research evidence for efficacy of yoga nidra

Research shows that yoga nidra is a safe, effective alternative or adjunct in the management of hypertension. Numerous trials have observed the influence of yoga nidra, and other relaxation practices derived from yoga nidra, in lowering the blood pressure, and their results have appeared in medical journals worldwide. All have shown significant responses, and today there is absolutely no doubt in scientific circles that yoga nidra effectively reduces tension and lowers blood pressure. It is only a matter of time before increasing tension levels, coupled with greater economic hardship in world communities, leads many more physicians to investigate and validate the practice of yoga nidra both for themselves and their hypertensive patients.

10

The research has been done. It is there for all to see and validate. The forthcoming introduction of yoga nidra into the standard medical treatment regime for hypertension in the next few years heralds one of the most significant revolutionary changes in medical therapeutics. It is beginning to occur now and it will continue. After its benefits in hypertension have been proved by more doctors, the rest will be plain sailing, because the benefits of yoga nidra and relaxation, as well as the other techniques of yoga, will be self-revealing and ongoing.

Dr Datey's study

Let me tell you about just one of the many important studies of yoga nidra. It was conducted at the Department of Cardiology at Bombay Hospital by one of India's most eminent cardiologists, Brigadier K.K. Datey, and first appeared in the journal *Angiology* in 1976.[4]

He trained 86 hypertensive men and women, average age 40 years, in yogic relaxation in shavasana (corpse posture). Their average blood pressure was 186/115 mm.Hg. The patients were divided into 3 groups. Group 1 contained patients who had not received any anti-hypertensive drug beforehand. Group 2 consisted of patients who had been taking anti-hypertensive drugs for at least two years, with adequate control of blood pressure. Group 3 were patients whose blood pressure remained inadequately controlled in spite of taking anti-hypertensive drugs. All patients were thoroughly trained in yogic relaxation at the cardiac clinic, and asked to continue to practise shavasana once or twice a day at home.

After three months, their clinical condition and blood pressure were reassessed. Significant results were recorded in all three groups. The majority of patients reported a general feeling of wellbeing, with marked improvement in symptoms like headache, insomnia and nervousness. In Group 1, average blood pressure dropped from 134 to 107 mm.Hg., a fall of 27 mm.Hg. In Group 2, average blood

11

pressure fell from 102 to 100 mm.Hg., but drug requirements were simultaneously reduced to 32% of the original dosage in 60% of patients. In Group 3, average blood pressure dropped from 120 mm.Hg. to 110 mm.Hg., while drug intake was simultaneously reduced to 29% of original levels in 38% of patients.

Furthermore, patients who failed to respond were generally those who were irregular in attendance and daily practice. These results are highly significant, and we can conclude that yoga nidra may well be the long sought after solution to the problem of hypertension. It clearly has value either in place of conventional drug therapies or in conjunction with them.

Further studies

Several other studies have produced comparable results. A study conducted at Stanford University School of Medicine, California, used 29 essential hypertensives who had been receiving medications for at least six months previously. They were divided into three groups. Group 1 received relaxation training directly from an instructor for ten weeks. Group 2 practised relaxation training at home with the aid of an audio-cassette recording. Group 3 underwent psycho-therapy without yogic relaxation training. At the six month follow-up, the therapist-conducted relaxation group fared best of all, revealing an average decrease of 7.8 mm.Hg. in systolic blood pressure and 9.7 mm.Hg. in diastolic blood pressure.[5] Similar results were obtained by other workers.[6]

Essential Hypertension and its Complications

Please speak about the application of yogic techniques in the management of hypertension and its complications, particularly the following specific types:
1. Essential juvenile hypertension
2. Hypertension with arteriosclerosis in the elderly
3. Hypertension with metabolic disturbances.

Hypertension is actually a symptom, and not a disease in its own right. However, it accompanies and complicates many disorders. The different terms or diagnostic tags associated with hypertension indicate specific pathological characteristics of individual cases in the spectrum of hypertension, including its likely prognosis. In prescribing yoga practices for the different degrees of hypertensive vascular degeneration, the best approach is to define a full program for simple hypertension and to modify this according to the various complications.

Arterial hypertension
Arterial hypertension refers to cases of essential hypertension uncomplicated by any other factors. No cause, beyond stress, can be detected, and it remains symptomless, except for an elevated blood pressure, at least in its early stages. Nevertheless, unless detected and controlled at an early stage, renal, arterial and cardiac damage will undoubtedly occur, with life expectancy reduced by years or

decades. Causes of death are most frequently stroke, heart failure or kidney failure.

Yogic management of simple hypertension
Please remember that all practices must be learned and practised under personal guidance from an expert.
1. *Relaxation*: Yoga nidra, including anuloma viloma and abdominal breath awareness, in shavasana.
2. *Asana*: Pawanmuktasana part 1 (anti-rheumatic), part 2 (digestive/abdominal) and part 3 (shakti bandhas), vajrasana series (particularly shashankasana and supta vajrasana), padmasana, yoga mudra and matsyasana.
3. *Pranayama*: Ujjayi, nadi shodhana, bhramari, sheetali, seetkari.
4. *Shatkriya*: Neti, laghoo shankhaprakshalana (if constipated). As the amount of water and salt may need adjusting, laghoo is best done only under expert guidance.
5. *Meditation*: Ajapa japa, antar mouna.
6. *Diet*: Salt reduction. Vegetarian diet free of excessive oil, spices, refined and processed foods. Evening meal should be small and light, and taken at sunset.
7. *Adequate exercise*: especially walking, and adequate rest.

Essential juvenile hypertension
Essential juvenile hypertension refers to an extreme form of essential hypertension in which the blood pressure rises suddenly and uncontrollably. It occurs usually in a young person. Although rare, it is frequently and rapidly fatal. It is also termed malignant hypertension. Blood pressure may be as high as 300/140 or more. It presents a medical emergency, as there is usually a sudden onset of blindness, giddiness, collapse, paralysis, etc.

Obviously, it demands immediate drug management, and intravenous vasodilators are usually prescribed. Subsequently, drug therapy should continue, but these cases prove notoriously difficult to control using drugs alone and frequently respond well to yoga nidra. This practice enables the sufferer to recognize gradually and resolve the suppressed unconscious impressions which are generating great tension as they seek to enter conscious awareness.

So, in cases of malignant hypertension, for acute management, intravenous anti-hypertensive agents are essential, and for long-term management, yoga nidra should be practised in conjunction with conventional drug management and close medical supervision and assessment. Other yoga practices can be gradually introduced once the blood pressure is under control.

Hypertension with arteriosclerosis in the elderly
Hypertension with arteriosclerosis is a late form of hypertension which proves most difficult to lower, whether by yogic or pharmacological means. It occurs where arterial hardening (arteriosclerosis) has developed over many years, generally due to undetected hypertension. It is usually seen in old people who remain untroubled and asymptomatic, even with blood pressures as high as 240/120. Once the arterial walls become permanently hardened, it is clear that a complete cure is no longer possible. The damage has already been done in preceding years. Vascular reactivity of hardened arteries (their ability to contract and dilate in response to signals from the hypothalamus) is reduced.

For these elderly persons, hypertension has become a way of life and they are often untroubled. Nevertheless, yoga nidra probably offers the best opportunity to remove cardiac strain and to prevent further degeneration and a sudden early demise. The pawanmuktasana part 1 series of exercises and nadi shodhana pranayama also prove valuable, but all strain should be avoided as the badly degenerated blood vessels make the occurrence of sudden deathly stroke or thromboembolism a real possibility.

Hypertension complicated by metabolic disturbances
Hypertension which is complicated by metabolic disturbances such as elevated blood lipid (fat) and cholesterol

15

levels (hypercholesterolemia), diabetes and thromboembolism are complex areas of medical management, where various metabolic and degenerative processes are precipitating or complicating a simple finding of elevated blood pressure. Here yogic management also becomes more complicated.

In cases of arteriosclerosis and hypertension, elevated blood lipid and cholesterol levels are frequent findings. In the past, obesity, lack of exercise and a high consumption of animal (saturated) fats in the diet have been implicated, and clearly a sensible yogic diet, free of excessive oils, dairy products and animal fats, should be adopted. Lower blood fat and cholesterol levels result and the rate of deposition of greasy and fatty materials (atheroma) onto the arterial walls decreases. There is even evidence to suggest that the deposition of fatty deposits can be reversed when a low fat diet is consumed, and a daily exercise program is followed.

However, cholesterol levels do not depend solely upon dietary fat intake. They have been found to be elevated in stressful conditions including public speaking, racing car driving and examinations.[1] They have also been found to be elevated in the serum of those who possess the typical coronary prone (type A) behaviour patterns of excessive aggression, competitiveness and self-assertion.[2] Studies at the University of Tel Aviv have shown that yogic relaxation practices (in this case transcendental meditation) lower the levels of cholesterol in the blood of hypercholesterolemic patients.[3] Researchers at Benares Hindu University have found that serum lipid levels are reduced in normal subjects taking a normal diet, following training in yogic asanas.[4]

The role of cholesterol

Cholesterol occupies a central position in the body's digestive, reproductive and cardiovascular metabolism. This fatty white substance is a precursor or building block in the synthesis of the steroid hormones by the liver, adrenal and reproductive glands. These vital hormones include:

16

- *Glucocorticoids* such as cortisone which act to mobilize the body's fuel supplies, thereby opposing the action of insulin and raising the concentration of sugar in the bloodstream.
- *Mineralocorticoids* such as aldosterone which maintain electrolyte balance in the body by altering the excretory mechanisms of the kidneys.
- *Sex hormones* (testosterone, oestrogen, progesterone) which are responsible for sexual characteristics and behaviour.

Therefore, cholesterol is definitely required by the body and if dietary sources are inadequate, it will be synthezised by the liver (endogenous cholesterol) and arterial deposits will also be used up. Thus, fasting and yoga may well reverse arterial cholesterol deposition.

When there are high levels of lipids and cholesterol in the blood, it becomes thick, turbid and milky. The serum (clear fraction of blood) of a heavy animal fat consumer is frequently milky in appearance, while that of a person on a low fat, vegetarian diet is clear. In hypercholesterolemia, deposition of fats in the walls of the vessels lead to arterial degeneration, and simultaneously, cardiac strain develops as the heart is forced to continually pump this heavy viscous blood.

Hypertension and diabetes

Diabetes refers to disturbance of the body's capacity to assimilate and utilize glucose. It is recognized as an elevated level of sugar in the blood. Diabetes frequently complicates cardiovascular degenerative diseases and it is known to accelerate hypertensive damage to the heart, blood vessels, eyes and kidneys. Diabetes is well recognized as a stress related disorder, and the blood sugar level is known to rise in conditions of emotional, environmental and intrapsychic stress. Diabetics have been shown to have higher levels of anxiety than the general population.[5] The end result is exhaustion of pancreatic secretory capacities and the clinical signs of diabetes – weakness, excessive thirst and urination, muscle wasting, resistant skin infections, etc. The eyesight is prone to degenerate in both hypertension and diabetes, and it is not surprising that the combination of an uncontrolled blood pressure and elevated blood sugar levels leads to visual degeneration and sudden or gradual blindness.

Yogic research in diabetes

Yogic management of diabetes is fairly well documented in Indian scientific literature. K.N. Udupa at Benares Hindu University has shown a lowering of blood sugar level in normal young volunteers after practising hatha yoga asanas and shatkriyas.[4] At the Scientific Seminars sponsored by the Central Council for Research in Indian Medicine in 1973 and 1975, successful clinical trials were reported. Dr Melkote of Lonavala (1973), Dr Varandani whose study was conducted at the Yoga Clinic and Hospital of Swami Anandananda in Jaipur (1973), and also Drs Rukmini and Sinha (1975) have all tabled most promising results.[6] Dr P.L. Lavgankar reported another successful trial in the Yoga Vidya Dham in Poona, directed by B.K.S. Iyengar.[7] In our own ashrams, a most successful trial was conducted at Bihar School of Yoga Calcutta Unit in 1976 under the supervision of Prof. N.C. Panda, head of the Department of Clinical Biochemistry at Sambalpur Medical College Hospital in Orissa.[8,9]

Yogic management of diabetes

The complete management program of diabetes is a whole topic on its own. Specific yogic practices must be prescribed, taking into account the individual patient's condition, and the diet must be carefully controlled. Of course, the blood sugar level must be serially monitored throughout the treatment and the dosages of anti-diabetic drugs such as insulin lowered carefully. Where the clinical picture is complicated by hypertension, the whole process becomes more complicated and great care is required. Treatment becomes more difficult because the more powerful yogic practices for diabetes are contraindicated in hypertension. Nevertheless, good results can be obtained, but progress is necessarily slower. In general, the more severe, longstanding and complicated is the pathology, the greater is the role of modern medical and surgical procedures. However, yoga still has a role to play.

Yoga's main role is preventative, and curative in the early stages of disease. Once major degeneration has set in, yoga's role becomes palliative and supportive. Then we prefer to work closely with the doctors, for pathology is primarily their field, while ours is health. Nevertheless, remarkable results sometimes occur even in severe and incurable diseases, because yoga is enormously powerful.

Recommended program for diabetes and hypertension

1. *Relaxation*: Practise yoga nidra intensively. It has been shown to lower both blood glucose and lipid levels by acting centrally upon the hypothalamus to reduce mental and intrapsychic imbalance in the autonomic nervous system. Always include abdominal breath awareness with counting and anuloma viloma.
2. *Asana*: Avoid surya namaskara and major asanas, but practise pawanmuktasana part 1 and part 2, gomukhasana, marjari-asana, vajrasana, shashankasana (static), rajju karshanasana, eka pada pranamasana.
3. *Pranayama*: Simple nadi shodhana, ujjayi and bhramari.
4. *Shatkriya*: Laghoo shankhaprakshalana and the full course of shankhaprakshalana should only be practised under strict guidance. Omit salt in shankhaprakshalana to avoid fluid and electrolyte imbalances.
5. *Correct diet* and meal timings. Adequate rest, exercise and sleep are essential.

Thromboembolism

Thromboembolism is a complication of severe and longstanding vascular degeneration. It often accompanies blood sugar and lipid disturbances and is a frequent cause of death in cardiovascular and hypertensive diseases. Thrombus refers to formation of blood clots on the walls of predamaged arteries and embolus refers to the breaking off of a blood clot and its movement through the bloodstream to lodge elsewhere in the arterial tree, where it frequently causes severe complications due to obstruction of blood flow there. This is a frequent cause of sudden death because clots lodge in the lungs (pulmonary embolism) or brain (cerebrovascular accident).

Recommended program for hypertension combined with thromboembolism

Patients suffering from hypertension with a past history of thromboembolism should practise a very light program in conjunction with conventional drug and dietary management of their condition. This will prevent any further degeneration. Because the blood vessels are in such a friable and delicate condition, care must be taken to avoid all strain in the practices. Yoga nidra, simple asanas from the pawanmuktasana part 1 series, and pranayamas such as ujjayi, nadi shodhana (without breath retention) and bhramari are ideal. A low fat, vegetarian diet should be adopted, which imposes minimal strain upon the heart and digestive organs. Nada yoga and kirtan are also important parts of yogic therapy for severe cardiovascular degeneration as they afford emotional release for the overburdened heart.

Question 4

Heart Disease

Degenerative heart disease is still a number one problem for the medical profession today. Existing research points to yoga as an effective relief with no negative side effects. What is your view of cardiovascular problems, and how can they be averted through the application of yoga?

Degenerative heart disease forms a whole spectrum of many stages and degrees of severity, with different and overlapping diagnostic tags. These include ischaemic heart disease (IHD). Ischaemia means degeneration due to lack of oxygen, and IHD refers to starvation of coronary muscles of oxygen. Cardiac pain arises solely due to ischaemia. When heart muscle is deprived of oxygen, it begins to die rapidly, giving rise to acute pain.

Where the deprivation is temporary; for example, when conditions of exercise or emotion cause the heart to accelerate and blood pressure to rise, there is a relative deficiency of oxygen reaching heart muscles in proportion to the higher demand. The extra blood required cannot be supplied because the coronary arteries, which branch from the aorta to supply blood to the heart muscle, have become narrow and constricted.

This pain is called angina pectoris – the classical chest pains which are relieved by rest and induced by physical or emotional activity. It is well recognized that both angina and heart attack frequently occur in dreaming sleep when

21

emotional content is being released on the mental and psychic planes.

Heart attack (also called myocardial infarction) is a more severe form of IHD. Here again, the process of oxygen deprivation is the source of pain, but now the obstruction to blood flow in one of the coronary muscles is complete. As a result, the muscle segment supplied by that artery dies. This pain is more severe, unrelenting and frequently radiates into the jaw, back and left arm. Whereas angina lasts two or three minutes, a heart attack lasts for hours or days if it remains untreated.

Heart attack is the most common cause of death in modern societies. However, some people survive heart attack and live for hours, days or years, depending on the site and extent of damage to the heart muscle. Sometimes the heart can limp on, continuing to pump, but if a crucial valve, node or part of the electrical conducting system of the heart has been destroyed, then the heartbeat will quickly become irregular (arrhythmia), resulting in failure to pump blood (cardiac failure), or in complete cessation of the heartbeat (asystole). After that, death is inevitable. However, if a non-essential section of cardiac muscle dies, the heart will continue to pump, albeit inefficiently.

A wide variety of drugs exist to bolster up a failing heart, tiding it over the period immediately following an attack, until collateral circulation of blood to the damaged area of heart muscle can be established. The crucial period of survival from a heart attack is the initial minutes, hours and days after it occurs. This is why those who quickly reach a coronary care unit where their complications can be managed, are far more likely to survive. Furthermore, one is more likely to die during the first heart attack than in any subsequent attacks.

Influence of testosterone on the male heart

Those who suffer from heart attack and angina at an early stage in life are usually found to be tense, ambitious, aggressive and 'successful', young or middle-aged men who work compulsively, eat, smoke and drink excessively and fail to exercise adequately. They often 'bottle up' their emotions internally, rarely expressing their innermost feelings, except in outbursts of anger, passion or violence. This has been termed the coronary prone or 'type A' personality.[1]

This pattern of behaviour is now believed to be induced by high levels of the male (androgenic) hormones such as testosterone. High doses of testosterone are known to promote aggression and type A behaviour in rats. Psychologists consider the same hormones to be responsible for the patterns of aggressive, highly competitive and sometimes violent behaviour which characterize the cardiac personality. Now it appears that testosterone directly influences the behaviour of the human heart as well.

Researchers at Texas University, San Antonio (USA) have recently discovered specific receptor sites for the androgenic hormones existing in the walls of the great arteries and heart chambers.[2] In conditions of excessive or uncontrolled liberation of testosterones into the bloodstream, the hormonal molecules appear to become affixed to these cardiac receptors, gradually 'wounding' the heart muscles and leading to heart disease at a premature age.

Many cardiologists, including Dr Christian Barnard, now recognize the value of yogic relaxation and practices such as siddhasana, which exert a stabilizing and harmonizing influence upon the emotional behaviour and endocrine secretion patterns. They commonly prescribe yogic asanas, meditation and relaxation as a means of protection against heart attack in middle and later life.

Coronary vasospasm

In the past, pathologists have always drawn a clear distinction between the temporary chest pains of angina and the severe and irreversible pains of a heart attack. Angina was considered to be due to the inability of hardened arteriosclerotic coronary arteries to dilate and supply the extra blood demanded by the cardiac muscle in conditions of exercise and emotional stress. Heart attack was considered to occur due to complete obstruction of a coronary artery by a thrombus (blood clot) generated in the artery itself or lodging there, after forming elsewhere in the arteriovenous tree (embolus), thus depriving a segment of cardiac muscle of its blood supply and leading to its death.

However, in clinical practice, no such sharp demarcation exists and it is often extremely difficult to diagnose whether a patient is undergoing an anginal attack or a major heart attack, especially in the first few minutes of onset of pain. The two clinical pictures differ only in the severity and duration, and frequently merge into one another. Medical science's traditional insistence that each is due to an entirely different cause has been disproved by various investigations.

Specifically, research from the University of Pisa (Italy) promises to revolutionize the whole management of acute cardiac pain.[3] Whereas cardiac pain was previously considered to be arising due to one of the irreversible factors of prior vessel hardening (angina) or blood clot formation (infarction), it has now been recognized that both angina and infarction form part of a single cardiac syndrome which arises due to a single mechanism – coronary vasospasm.

Coronary vasospasm refers to a state of partial or complete spasm of coronary arteries due to factors of emotional or psychic tension being relayed from the thinking (cortical) and feeling (limbic) areas of the brain, through the hypothalamic control centre to the walls of the coronary blood vessels via the sympathetic (vasoconstrictive) nerve fibres. The arteriosclerotic hardening to which angina is attributed may be present beforehand, and the clot formation to which heart attack is attributed probably occurs afterwards (even as a post mortem event). But at the instant of actual attack and pain, the initiating event is a potentially reversible nervous spasm of the coronary arteries. We can conclude that yoga nidra, which instantly defuses psychic tension and conflict, and induces a state of mental peace and emotional relaxation in trained practitioners, has the capacity to rapidly reverse coronary vasospasm, alleviate anginal pain and avert potential myocardial infarction at the instant of its onset.

The role of yoga nidra

Yoga relaxation and meditation have been shown to effectively influence the cause of heart disorders by reducing the effect of stressful environmental and intrapsychic factors upon the sympathetic nervous system.[4] In the field of heart disease, the practice is emerging as an effective preventative, curative and palliative in all degrees of heart strain and failure, from the acute infarction situation when death is imminent, to the patient with long-standing angina, cardiac insufficiency and failure, who limps on at home as a 'cardiac cripple'. Relaxation has been shown to lower the heart rate, decrease the blood pressure and relieve the working strain upon the cardiac muscles.[5]

In the preventive situation, yoga nidra counteracts heart strain by inducing a more relaxed mental attitude and emotional climate, enabling its practitioner to better withstand the stresses of daily life. It has also been shown to reduce many of the risk factors implicated in heart disease, including elevated levels of circulating cholesterol, lipids, glucose, lactate, aldosterone, testosterone and noradrenaline in the bloodstream.

Patients who practise yoga nidra daily soon become competent in defusing intrapsychic and emotional tension alone and unaided. This is an invaluable skill in modern life. Those who possess it have a great power at their disposal. They are capable of averting a heart attack. In the past, one was suddenly rendered a 'helpless victim' of heart attack. This attitude of helplessness was encouraged by the medical establishment, which had not understood the value of yogic techniques for relieving and averting the incipient heart attack or bout of angina. However, this attitude is changing rapidly, and it is becoming increasingly well-known that the incidence and outcome of heart attack is not strictly predetermined.

The cardiac neurosis

Many cardiac patients develop fear because they are lacking the vital knowledge of how to survive a heart attack. They feel they have no power or control over their own thoughts and feelings and that damage to their hearts is therefore inevitable. This fear is in turn a major factor precipitating cardiac incidents. At the first sign of slight palpitations, which are normal events in the lives of most people, those who are fearful for their cardiac health become so frightened that they precipitate an attack of emotional angina or even a full heart attack as a direct result. This is a well-recognized medical syndrome, termed cardiac neurosis.

Millions suffer from this syndrome today. It has no biological basis, and clinical and electrocardiogram (ECG) findings reveal a 'normal' heart. Yet the sufferer lives a life of paralyzing anxiety, remaining in constant fear of imminent death. This fear and helplessness are often over-powering and such patients can never accept reasonable reassurances that their heart is normal in every way. Fear and helplessness are major precipitators of acute heart attack, while diet, obesity, smoking, etc. play a less significant role in comparison. This is why yoga nidra is the most important single practice of all in preventing and alleviating heart attack.

The patient who is familiar with yoga nidra and practices it daily will become more and more proficient at averting this 'fearful victim' complex each time it arises into their conscious awareness. They will learn to recognize and witness the reactions of fear, self-pity, rage, etc., as they occur, and to stop identifying with them. This is the fundamental principle of yogic management of heart attack and it proves highly effective.

Conventional management of myocardial infarction

The medical management of heart attack and its subsequent complications is a highly complex field, and coronary care is surely one of the most exciting and successful spheres of modern medical science. Studies have shown that the sooner the patient is delivered into a coronary care unit, the more likely they are to survive the heart attack. Many drugs and procedures may be adopted to bolster a failing heart. Included are:

- Analgesics like morphine for pain relief.
- Cardiac resuscitation by either electrical, chemical or manual means, if the heart stops altogether (asystole). Drugs used include atropine and adrenalin.
- Oxygen.
- Vasodilators to open up the blood vesels and reduce the load on the heart.
- Sedatives for anxiety.
- Electrocardiogram (ECG) and continuous monitoring of the cardiac impulse.
- Defibrillation by electrical means and control of arrhythmias, using drugs (digitalis, lignocaine, isoprenaline, propanolol, etc.) to restore normal (sinus) rhythm where a rapid or irregular heartbeat and subsequent heart failure has developed.

Yogic alternative

Yoga nidra is the only yogic practice which should be adopted during the major cardiac crisis. Yoga nidra is a state of altered awareness in which extreme relaxation prevails. The patient should be led into the state of yoga nidra by an experienced guide. This should occur at the site of initial collapse, during resuscitation in the ambulance, and most importantly, in the coronary care unit itself. The most ideal situation is when the doctor and nurses are highly trained and proficient in yoga therapy. Then the whole emergency procedure can proceed while the patient remains in the yoga nidra state of deeply relaxed, attentive

27

awareness. When the patient is practising yoga nidra, an intrapsychic communion is created between patient and therapist, and this vastly enhances any other therapeutic procedures being administered.

By powerfully diverting the patient's attention to the flow of breath in the nostrils (anuloma viloma) or the rise and fall of the navel (abdominal breath and ajapa japa), there will be a continuous defusion of incipient fear and anxiety states. Release of vasospasm can thus be attained and heart attack averted. This state of yoga nidra can be maintained for many hours, if necessary, in the hands of a skilled therapist. It enables the patient to consciously avert his awareness, thus controlling the coronary state.

Periodically, the patient should be roused from yoga nidra and encouraged to develop awareness of the physical body and the circulation of blood and prana within it. For this purpose, the pawanmuktasana exercises for the hands and feet are ideal. These avoid total dissociation of the patient's conscious awareness and prana (life force) from the physical body, which is usually the sign of physical death. In the dream-like state of yoga nidra, physical consciousness often diminishes, yet awareness remains intact. Do not forget that during heart attack, the patient is in the lap of death, but if he possesses the threshold awareness of yoga nidra, he need not become death's victim. Then he has a choice. There is no reason why the whole coronary care process could not be conducted with the patient's aid and awareness using yoga nidra. But the doctors must first learn and practise yoga nidra themselves in order to experience firsthand how it defuses anxiety.

Passive and dynamic relaxation

The acute coronary sufferer can gain enormous benefit from a combination of specific asanas, pranayamas, and passive and active relaxation techniques. In our ashrams we teach yoga nidra as a passive system of deep relaxation, while we also adopt nada yoga techniques where a sustained

28

state of more dynamic relaxation is required, such as in the days and weeks following a major coronary incident. During this period the most important task is to promote the optimal self-healing conditions and capacities of cardiac tissues by relieving them of the constant physiological burden which accompanies high anxiety, stress and worry. We find nada yoga techniques are an ideal way of holding these anxieties at bay and providing emotional relaxation.

Recommended program for cardiac care

1. *Asana*: The patient should be resting either in shavasana or in the 'coronary posture', a variation of utthanpadasana, where the head and legs are slightly elevated from the bed by pillows. This posture is also a modified form of vipareeta karani asana. These are the only two postures which simultaneously give rest to the heart (reduced heart rate) and improve cardiac performance by enhancing venous return and cardiac output.[6]

No other major asanas are indicated at this crucial stage of decreased cardiac performance. All strain is contra-indicated as cardiac reserve capacity does not exist, and the heart is either failing or on the verge of slipping into failure. However, there are a few simple exercises for the limbs which can be performed periodically throughout the crucial period. The pawanmuktasana part 1 series, when practised with awareness, exert a powerful influence upon peripheral circulation of blood and lymphatic fluids. They also stimulate the origins and terminations of the nadis or pathways of psychic energy which arise in the fingers and toes and are responsible for the balanced and integrated function of all the internal organs.

The existence of these nadis, which are known as meridians in Chinese and oriental medicine, has been clearly demonstrated by the experiments of Dr Hiroshi Motoyama in Japan[7], while the discoveries of Kirlian photography give tangible photographic evidence of the prana, chi or bioplasmic energy flowing within the nadis.

29

2. *Yoga nidra*: In cardiac care, the first and foremost practice is initiation into yogic relaxation. The whole experience of yogic relaxation has to be conveyed by a highly skilled doctor or yoga therapist to the sufferer, who is usually completely beset by fears about their heart, their family, their business and so many other things. Once it has been successfully conveyed and mastered by the sufferers themselves, they can confidently short circuit the enormous load of anxiety they are carrying, and enter into a more relaxed state of being. This state is crucial in cardiac recovery.

3. *Nada yoga*: Termed the 'yoga of sound'. It is a means of transcending the mundane, gross, material consciousness in order to become aware of the underlying vibrational (sound) essence of all creation. This yoga begins with an awareness of sound.

In nada yoga you are aware of the mantra or the sound, and just that. You concentrate on the sound and trace it to its very source (bindu). As you know, sound vibration has a very powerful influence upon the mind because it takes place at a purely intuitive, feeling level which bypasses any intellectual analysis. Sound and music are the media of emotion. We feel them in this way. This is how nada yoga effectively renders the intellect incapable of its normal operation and channels the emotions positively, away from the finite, personal or individual obsessions and into the impersonal, cosmic and universal dimension. In a fearful, tense, neurotic or guilt-ridden mind, this brings an instant relief of tension which is soothing, relaxing and totally absorbing.

In the practice of nada yoga, specific mantras can be chanted or silently intoned. The musical scales of a harmonium can also be used very effectively, creating harmony between voice and musical note. The patient follows the sound as he rests comfortably in the 'coronary posture'. In this way, the deepest experience of physical, mental, emotional and cardiac relaxation is achieved, and it can go on for hours and days. Another approach is for the instructor to chant the mantra Om, requesting the patient to let go of all preconceptions and ideas and just follow the sound, absorbing himself within its vibration.

In India, we utilize the classical system of Indian music or ragas. The mood of each raga corresponds to the various periods of day and night, and harmonizes with the cyclical nature of hormonal secretion and physiological activity in the 24 hour period. Each raga is divinely inspired, aimed towards liberating the individual's awareness into the spiritual dimension in a very subtle way. It is the aural expression of the daily cycle of life in India.

Whatever type of music you choose, there is one very important thing to remember: the channel of emotional expression which is created by the music must be an expansive, liberating one, leading to the divine source. The romantic, passionate type of music which is popular today is unsuitable here because it reflects emotions and moods that are constrictive and personally directed. These songs of jealousy, lust, anger, passion, self-pity, infatuation, betrayal, etc. have often been the cause of heart pain. How can they bring relief from it? The music must elevate and liberate the awareness away from self-obsession.

Question 5

Cardiac Arrhythmias and the Unstable Pacemaker

What are the yogic techniques used in the management of cardiac arrhythmias (heart rhythm disturbances), and in controlling an unstable pacemaker (s.a. node)?

Defining the normal heart

Arrhythmia refers to a disturbance of the cardiac impulse, and is one of the most frequent complications of cardiac ischaemia, heart attack and circulatory failure. In a healthy individual, the heartbeat is regular in both time and amplitude. Its normal range is from 60–90 beats per minute, but it may rise to 100–120 or more during severe exercise or high anxiety.

On the other hand, in hatha yogis and trained athletes who undergo a specific process of cardiorespiratory training, especially swimmers, the pulse rate at rest may drop as low as 50 or even 40 per minute. If we add to this the research studies conducted upon some yogis who have demonstrated the capacity to stop and restart their hearts at will, then it becomes clear that the range of 'normal' behaviour of the human heart and its possibilities have not been fully explored at the present time.[1,2,3]

Nevertheless, two conclusions can be drawn:
1. The behaviour of the heart can be voluntarily influenced to a variable degree through systematic cardiorespiratory training.

2. The human heart is not an independent organ which fails spontaneously, of its own accord. Heart disease is an effect of an imbalance or loss of control elsewhere, in the hypothalamus and vasomotor centres of the brain. This imbalance is relayed to the heart via the sympathetic (excitatory) nerves, resulting in an accelerated pulse (tachycardia) and an unstable coronary impulse (arrhythmia).

The origin of the cardiac impulse

The human heart beats of its own volition from the third month of intrauterine life up until the last breath. During this time, which may even span one hundred years, the heart appears to neither rest nor tire. Even as all other cells and tissues of the body demand physiological rest and rejuvenation during sleep, this unique neuromuscular pump beats on relentlessly.

Experiments have shown that the cardiac impulse originates spontaneously from the sino-atrial (s.a.) node or pacemaker, a delicate piece of neuromuscular tissue embedded in the muscular wall of the right atrium, the smallest of the four heart chambers. This tiny isolated focus possesses remarkable and unique properties, for it is the only group of cells in the body which spontaneously generates its own inherent electrical impulses. Not one of the billions of neurons of the brain possesses this independent and spontaneous self-generating capacity. This surely highlights the contention of many realized yogis and jnanis, such as Ramana Maharshi, who insisted that the real seat of the atman, personal soul or individual spark of consciousness is to be experienced within the heart, and not in the complexity of the brain, which is only the seat of the hypnotic yet illusory veil of the ego.

The spark of life

The sino-atrial node initiates a tiny spark-like electrical impulse 70 times per minute. This becomes the initiative

33

stimulus for the subsequent contraction of the heart, which sends blood coursing throughout the body fuelling every vital organ and process, including the brain. The impulse from this node is conducted almost instantaneously throughout the heart via a network of nervous conducting fibres within the cardiac muscle. Within only a few milliseconds, the whole cardiac muscle is electrically depolarized. This wave of depolarization is followed an instant later by a wave of muscular contraction (systole), as the heart's two larger muscular chambers or ventricles, simultaneously pump venous blood from the body to the lungs through the right chambers, and arterial blood from the lungs into the aorta and arterial tree through the left chambers.

Immediately following ventricular contraction within the cardiac cycle, there is a rest period (diastole) during which the heart muscles relax, the electrical conducting network is repolarized and the chambers again fill with blood. This cardiac cycle is repeated 70 times per minute in the healthy resting heart.

Is arrhythmia physiological or pathological?

Arrhythmias arise in many different physiological and pathological situations. The most fundamental arrhythmia (sinus arrhythmia) is a normal accompaniment of the respiratory cycle. It can hardly be considered pathological, unless the process of cyclical respiration and of individual consciousness itself is to be recognized for what it is, a diseased condition, by virtue of its illusiveness and impermanence. According to yogic texts and tradition, the complete suspension of respiration (kevala kumbhaka) is one accompaniment of the highest states of samadhi, where the illusory veil of the ego is forever rent asunder. The being who emerges from that samadhi is a jivanmukta and is liberated from all sense of personal identification with the body, breath or mind.

Whether sinus arrhythmia is to be considered as physiological or pathological is for you to decide.

34

Nevertheless, it is the departure point for the whole range of progressively more severe arrhythmias which reflect increasingly poor adaptation to the stresses of life. The next arrhythmia is sinus tachycardia, a simple accelerated heart rate in the range of 90–150 beats per minute. Is it physiological or pathological? Again it is difficult for a yogi to answer. You may say that it is physiological if it is induced by exercise and pathological if it is caused by anxiety.

The more serious disruptions of cardiac rhythm are those in the domain of conventional pathology. Arrhythmias such as extra systoles may be early signs of cardiac ischaemia or some other metabolic imbalance, while atrial or ventricular fibrillations are severe, life-threatening arrhythmias which usually arise only in the hours of cardiac shock and electrolyte and circulatory imbalance following a heart attack. Some of the causes of arrhythmias are: anxiety (including 'cardiac neurosis'), oxygen starvation (hypoxia and ischaemia), acidosis and disordered electrolyte balance, especially of potassium and calcium. Some arrhythmias can be diagnosed on clinical examination of the pulse, but electrocardiogram tracing is far more precise.

Classification of arrhythmias

1. *Sinus rhythm*: These are the simpler physiological disturbances of rate, with no other defects of electrical conduction.

   a) *Sinus tachycardia*: A simple accelerated heart rate (usually inferior to 150 beats per minute) caused by exercise, anxiety or drugs. Also occurs in fever and infectious conditions, or may be caused by excessive tea, coffee, tobacco, alcohol, drugs such as atropine and adrenaline, etc.

   b) *Sinus bradycardia* (slow heart rate): Usually inferior to 60 beats per minute with regular rhythm. Seen normally in some athletes.

   c) *Sinus arrhythmia*: This is a normal arrhythmia, referring to the change of heart rate within the respiratory cycle – with inspiration, rate increases; with expiration, rate decreases.

2. *Extra systoles* (ectopic beats): These are the first truly pathological arrhythmias, usually due to ischaemia heart disease. Here extra impulses intrude irregularity into the regular sinus rhythm. In the pulse they are felt as irregular beats. They arise from a source other than the sino-atrial node (ectopic focus). The ectopic source may be atrial or ventricular. These are not severe disturbances of cardiac conduction, but may herald an impending severe arrhythmia.

3. *Tachycardias*: These refer to greatly accelerated heart rates which seriously disrupt cardiac output and lead to circulatory failure.

   a) *Paroxysmal atrial tachycardia*: Refers to bursts of accelerated heart rate of an abrupt onset and cessation. Rate is superior to 150 per minute. Common in IHD.

   b) *Atrial fibrillation*: Atrial contraction at a rate of 340–600 contractions per minute. Pulse is irregular, with missed (dropped) beats. Common arrhythmia seen in IHD.

   c) *Ventricular fibrillation*: Ventricles in a spasm of rapid, ineffective pulsations. This is heart failure, as the heart's ability to pump the blood is lost. A terminal event.

4. *Disorders of conduction*: These are due to blockage in the nerve conduction pathways by which the depolarizing coronary impulse is conducted throughout the heart muscles. Usual causes are ischaemia or infarction of the nerve pathways. They include:

   a) *Sino-atrial block*: electrical isolation of the sino-atrial node.

   b) *Atrio-ventricular block*: partial or complete blockage of electrical impulses into ventricles.

   c) *Bundle-branch block* (right or left): selective electrical blockage of right or left conducting pathways.

Medical management of arrhythmias

These cardiac arrhythmias demand management according to the degree to which they affect the circulation. Some are normal (e.g. sinus tachycardia, sinus arrhythmia), while others are pathological but relatively harmless (e.g. isolated extra systoles). Still others lead to failure of the heart to effectively pump blood, and circulatory failure and death commonly result.

Drug management of arrhythmias is a complex and delicate process. Many powerful drugs are used in an effort to stabilize the impulse and restore effective circulation. Overdosage is a dangerous possibility, and many times one pattern of arrhythmia may be controlled, only to be superseded by another pattern. In this way, an unstable heart can flutter from one arrhythmia to another for hours, days or weeks immediately following an infarct, while the patient's life remains in the balance throughout.

Yogic management of arrhythmias

Yoga definitely has a major role to play in management of cardiac arrhythmias of all degrees of severity. I believe that as long as the patient remains conscious, he is able to exert a profound controlling influence over an irregular and unstable coronary impulse, provided he is aware of a few yogic practices. The first is yoga nidra and the second is nadi shodhana pranayama.

Each of these practices exerts a precise and distinct physiological action upon coronary behaviour. When they are combined in acute coronary medicine, the two practices complement each other. Nadi shodhana acts directly to stabilize the fundamental rhythmic cycle of the cardio-respiratory system, while yoga nidra acts centrally upon the hypothalamus, influencing the influx of stressful stimuli upon the heart via the sympathetic nerves. In acute coronary management they are combined together into one practice which is known as anuloma viloma.

37

Nadi shodhana: the 'coronary pranayama'

Nadi shodhana pranayama (alternate nostril breathing) is the first and fundamental pranayama in all yoga sadhana. It forms the basis of yoga's systematic training of the cardiorespiratory system. In yoga therapy, nadi shodhana forms the basic framework for coronary stability and cardiorespiratory health, and from the spiritual viewpoint, this pranayama is the departure point for meditation (dhyana yoga).

To understand how nadi shodhana influences cardiac behaviour, we have to discuss the nature of the cardiac and respiratory ratios. The heart's phenomenal capacity to beat continuously 70 times per minute, 24 hours a day, 365 days a year, for 70 or more years, makes it unique amongst all the body tissues. It is possible because of the unique nature of the heart's rhythm of systole/diastole or contraction/relaxation.

The time of cardiac contraction (systole) is half the duration of the relaxatory phase of the cycle (diastole). During diastole, the heart muscles rest momentarily and the ratio of exertion/rest is 1:2. This means that the heart actually gains a short rest during each diastolic period. This form of cyclical rest is unique to heart muscle, unlike other tissues such as the brain or skeletal muscles. The brain is active for extended periods, but gains rest at night during REM (dreaming) and deep sleep. Similarly, the skeletal muscles labour continuously during physical work, but relax deeply and efficiently during yoga asanas or sleep. The heart can afford no such luxury, so it gains its rest momentarily in the diastolic period between each ventricular contraction. Even though it pumps continuously, it actually works for only 8 hours of the day and rests for 16 hours. This is the natural rhythm of the healthy, normal heart.

Nadi shodhana is used to bolster this natural rhythm, which ensures continuous adequate rest for the heart. In cases where the sinus rhythm of the pacemaker has become unstable or has even been completely usurped, nadi

38

shodhana is the single most powerful practice to re-establish the natural order. Its action is as powerful as many drugs, and if your patients use this 'coronary pranayama' consciously, you will find you need far lower dosages to maintain coronary equilibrium and stability.

In this practice, the ratio of inhalation to exhalation is 1:2. After training, the respiration of a yogi automatically retains this ratio. In pranayama, more oxygen may be inhaled, but that is not the important point. If oxygenation alone were the purpose, then deep breathing exercises would be sufficient, but yogic pranayama is more subtle in its effects. Inhalation and exhalation must be trained in the ratio 1:2, because this ratio is most beneficial for the heart. How can this be? If you observe the pulse, you will see that with inspiration the heart speeds up, while with exhalation it slows down. In fact, this is the most fundamental of all the arrhythymias, sinus arrythmia – a normal, physiological event, not a pathological one.

Therefore, when the ratio 1:2 is practised, the overall effect is to relax the coronary muscles, but not at the cost of reducing the blood supply to the brain and body tissues. The crucial ratio of 1:2 is the yogic secret of mental health and physical rejuvenation. You may say, would it not be even better if we can attain 1:4? But then you are cancelling out the relaxation effect, because the brain accelerates the heart rate in reaction to a decreased supply of oxygen in the blood, and this is what occurs if expiration is further prolonged.

The ratio between respiration and pulse is a very important index of health. It should be in the ratio of 4 heartbeats for every breath. This means about 70 heartbeats and 15 breaths per minute. Proper timing is one of the best indications of good health.

Dr G. von Hildebrandt of the University of Marburg (Germany) has found that cardiac patients often have a speeded up and disrupted cycle, so that the ratio of heartbeat to breath approaches 6:1.[4] Disruption of this ratio in the earlier years of life is an almost certain indication of incipient cardiac disease in the later years, for it means that the heart is being robbed of its rest continually and will ultimately become prematurely exhausted, leading to heart failure. Hildebrandt uses a program of spa therapy (natural baths), regular hours of rest, simple diet and programmed exercise and activity to restore a wayward 6:1 rhythm back towards 4:1. In many ways it resembles the regular and scheduled lifestyle which we follow in ashram life.

We can conclude that nadi shodana should be further investigated in cardiac medicine without delay.

Mind and breath are mirrors
As clinicians you must all be aware of the relationship between the state of mind and the cardiac and respiratory rates. If you consider those of your patients who are prime candidates for heart attack – the anxious, highly-strung, ambitious, compulsive personalities, what is the status of their breath? Is it not fast and laboured? Inspiration/ expiration is nowhere near 1:2. It is more likely 1:1, and may even be reversed to 2:1. Similarly their cardiosrespiratory ratio is surely deviated from 4:1 further towards 6:1. In yogic science, these are clear indicators of poor health and impending calamity. They are also a clear indication of the state of that patient's level of mental control and awareness. When the mind is full of restless desire, ambitions, emotions, anxiety, fear and so on, the breath is agitated, rapid and uncontrolled, and the heart rate is accelerated and prone to palpitations. Are these not the very mental states in which anginal pain strikes, and heart attack occurs? There is a direct relationship between breath and mind; they are mirrors of one another, and when the breath is controlled the anarchical mind is harnessed.

Regular breathing induces relaxation, regularity and integration of the body's rhythms and processes so that they work together in harmony. Irregular breathing is a feature of dangerous mental frameworks, anxiety, chaotic thinking patterns, hysteria and disordered living. It accompanies physical, emotional and mental blockage, conflicts, impulsiveness and disease. Without awareness of breath or mind, we readily slip into these unhealthy patterns and behaviours. The need for the practice of breath awareness and control was highlighted by the German psychiatrist Wilhelm Reich, who stated, "There is no neurotic individual who is capable of exhaling completely in a single breath, deeply and evenly."

In yoga therapy, we place a high emphasis on pranayama in both cure of cardiac diseases, and more importantly, in their prevention. We recommend 10 or 15 minutes of nadi shodhana be practised each morning as a prelude to japa or meditation and after performing a few asanas. This cardiorespiratory training plays a fundamental role in preventing the inroads of degenerative stress related to diseases of modern life. If you initiate your cardiac patients into nadi shodhana, you will be delivering them from an early cardiac death. If you teach your arrhythmic patients to breathe attentively in the 1:2 ratio, you will find it exerts an immediate stabilizing influence upon their fluctuating heart rhythm. Stages 1 and 2 of nadi shodhana are sufficient, but there should be just a slight pause between inspiration and expiration.

Nadi shodhana averts infarction

In 1948, American cardiologist Dr Aaron Friedell reported in the journal *Minnesota Medicine* that anginal pain and imminent infarction can be averted by a form of breathing he called 'automatic attentive breathing'.[5] This was actually the first stage of nadi shodhana, and he found it extremely effective.

In yoga therapy we have also found that attentive breathing, as in nadi shodhana pranayama, will avert an anginal attack or infarct, even as it is occurring. Whenever pain arises, cardiac patients should stop whatever they are doing, thinking or feeling and turn their attention to their breathing, while at the same time endeavouring to keep themselves fully at ease and relaxed.

In the rehabilitative situation

After infarction another practice is recommended as a means of increasing cardiac reserves. First the patient diverts the attention to outside sounds, listening attentively to the singing of a bird in a nearby tree, or some other specific, isolated external sound.

The next step is to fix the awareness upon the inflowing and outflowing breath as the vehicle of relaxation. The respiration should be in ujjayi (slow, diaphragmatic inhalation). This occurs spontaneously when the tongue is turned back with its undersurface against the palate (khechari mudra). Ujjayi is correct if there is a slight internal snoring sound produced by the flowing breath in the throat area. This sound is produced internally and may be imperceptible to anyone close by. It resembles the snoring sound produced by an infant during sleep.

Inspiration in ujjayi should be slow and deep as the diaphragm descends into the abdomen. This is correct when the navel moves slowly outwards. It should be followed by a slight pause. In this way the breathing cycle continues with the patient's awareness absorbed within it.

We have devised this 'coronary pranayama' from our experiences with many sufferers of coronary insufficiency who have attended our ashram for yoga therapy. It is invariably extremely effective. It is actually a combination of several tantric practices, including antar mouna (developing witness awareness), ajapa japa (ascent and descent of breath awareness between the throat and navel with ujjayi breathing) and nadi shodhana pranayama.

In the rehabilitation situation, nadi shodhana or alternate nostril breathing should be performed in a sitting position with the spine erect in order to improve the diaphragmatic descent in ujjayi. First the right nostril is closed off and the breath enters and leaves via the left

42

nostril alone. This continues for 10 complete breaths. Always the left nostril is first, as this activates the parasympathetic limb of the autonomic nervous system (ida nadi) and brings immediate mental relaxation and internal absorption. Then we close the left nostril and open the right one (pingala nadi) and 10 more complete deep breaths in ujjayi are performed. This externalizes the awareness and activates the flow of pranic energy (life force) in the network of nadis (nerve channels) throughout the body. In medical science, this nadi is termed the sympathetic nervous system.

In acute infarction
If the coronary pain arises at night during sleep, nadi shodhana should be performed slightly differently. It is not even necessary to sit up; shavasana should be adopted, allowing the whole body to relax and settle itself down. Then the awareness is directed towards the flow of breath entering and leaving the nostrils. There is a subtle experience of breath flowing in and out of the nostrils and this must be witnessed closely. This breath may be experienced in a triangular pattern, with the sides of the triangle in the two nostrils and the apex at the eyebrow centre (bhru-madhya). The inflowing breath passes up from the nostrils to the eyebrow centre, and the outflowing breath flows from the eyebrow centre down through the nostrils. This practice of nadi shodhana carried out entirely on the mental and psychic plane in yoga nidra is called *anuloma viloma*.

The breath of life
We have taught the coronary pranayama to many patients who were 'cardiac cripples' and it has soon become automatic with them. Whenever they encounter the stressful situations which precipitate cardiac pain, they simply resort to the practice and gain relief. Within a few weeks their whole outlook changes. As they become completely confident and secure with the practice their former fears are discarded.

43

Often they are able to discontinue their drug therapies and readopt a normal life and full employment, free from the fear of pain. It is only necessary to restrict their activities as a sensible precautionary measure, and to perform the pranayama for a few minutes two or three times a day.

Question 6

Stroke

In rehabilitation from stroke, to what extent can lost brain function be restored through application of yoga?
Both yogic and modern medical scientists have concerned themselves with the problems of degeneration and deficiency of the human brain, and each science has developed its own particular conceptions about this enormous problem, as well as its own techniques and prescriptions to restore and even to enhance brain function. If we can succeed in merging these two approaches, a better fundamental understanding of the normal and abnormal brain will surely emerge, together with a more enlightened therapeutic approach.

The medical viewpoint
Medical science is mainly concerned with the pathology of severe brain deficiency and impairment, and focuses its attention upon the management and treatment of the major, acute and terminal brain disturbances known as stroke or cerebrovascular accident (CVA). Strokes are the third most common cause of death in developed societies, following cardiovascular degeneration and cancer. In fact, stroke is also a degenerative vascular disorder, arising out of the same arteriosclerotic process as coronary vascular disease; the only difference is that now the focus of degeneration is the delicate blood supply to the brain. The brain's blood

45

vessels are not spared from the generalized arterial damage induced by arteriosclerosis, hypertension, etc. Rather, they are prime targets because the neurons of the brain and central nervous system are believed to be incapable of replicating or regenerating after injury or oxygen deprivation, and are therefore uniquely vulnerable amongst all the body cells and tissues. Brain cells die after only 3 minutes of oxygen deprivation and this death results in irretrievable loss of various mental faculties and neurological capacities.

Causes of stroke

Predisposing factors to stroke include hypertension, heart disease, diabetes, raised serum lipids (fats) and smoking. Stroke victims are usually above 60 years of age and their sex incidence is equal. Immediate precipitating causes are:

1. *Arteriosclerotic degeneration* of the cerebral blood vessels, leading to decreased oxygen supply (hypoxia) to the various areas of the brain, or to haemorrhage into the brain itself. The brain receives its blood supply via four major arteries:
   a) *Internal carotid arteries* (right and left) entering the base of the brain via the side of the neck;
   b) *Vertebral arteries* (right and left) entering the posterior brain alongside the spinal cord. These four arteries meet in an anastomotic ring surrounding the pituitary gland at the base of the brain (the Circle of Willis), and from this circle, the arteries which carry blood to the various parts of the brain emerge.

2. *Hypertension* where high blood pressure leads to blowout (aneurysm) of a cerebral artery, with haemorrhage into the brain matter.

3. *Embolism* from the heart in myocardial infarction, rheumatic heart disease, etc. Here a blood clot or some other material lodges in the artery of the brain, leading to death of the dependent brain tissues.

4. *Other causes* include syphilis, cerebral vein thrombosis and drugs such as oral contraceptives.

46

Symptoms of stroke

The symptoms of stroke vary, depending on the severity and site of the accident in the brain and also upon its stage of development. The onset of a major stroke may be sudden or gradual. Symptoms may include sudden collapse or gradual loss of consciousness, increasing headache, dizziness, blindness, loss of speech, loss of control of voluntary functions such as urination, and paralysis or weakness of one side of the body.

Chances of survival

The chances of survival from a stroke depend on two factors:
1. *The level of consciousness*: Eighty-seven per cent of comatose patients die within 3 weeks of stroke onset, compared to only 24% of those who remain alert. Clouding of consciousness, amnesia, unilateral paralysis, blindness, aphasia (loss of speech) and dementia are common sequelae of a completed stroke. These symptoms are often partially or even completely reversible in the days or weeks following a stroke, but a high proportion of sufferers remain permanently afflicted mentally and physically, and a significant proportion never regain more than vegetal consciousness, living in a semi-conscious, comatose state with minimal external awareness.
2. *The precise pathology*: The immediate mortality rate has been estimated to be 90% from intracerebral haemorrhage, 60% from embolism and 37% from cerebral thrombosis.

Of every 10 stroke sufferers admitted to hospital, 3 will usually die, 2 will remain crippled, while 5 will recover their faculties partially or completely.

Classification of stroke

Strokes can be classified according to their stage of development:
1. *Completed stroke* means stroke has reached its maximum within 6 hours of its onset.

2. *Progressive stroke* continues to develop over a period of 6 hours to a few days, usually due to continuing intracerebral haemorrhage.
3. *Mini-strokes* or transient ischaemic attacks (TIAs) are transient focal disturbances of neurological function. The attack lasts less than 24 hours and symptoms revert spontaneously. Symptoms depend on site of origin of the lesion, but commonly include transient paralysis and loss of sight or speech capacities. There is often a temporary derangement of consciousness, with failure to recognize familiar faces, etc. One or more TIAs often precede a major stroke.

Medical management of acute stroke

The medical management of the comatose stroke patient in the acute phase includes:
• Maintenance of a clear airway, preventing the tongue from falling back into the throat and obstructing respiration.
• Placing patient in lateral 'unconscious' position.
• Frequent change of posture.
• Urinary catherization.
• Fluid maintenance by nasogastric tube or intravenous line.
• Passive movement of limbs regularly.

Clearly yoga plays no precise role here, as a functional personal awareness is absent. Good nursing care is most important.

Prognosis and rehabilitation after stroke

Of stroke survivors:
• 55% will be rehabilitated, perhaps with some minor residual disability.
• 20% will be able to walk without help but will have some major disability.
• 15% will require help to walk.
• 10% will remain crippled.

Rehabilitation begins the moment the patient gains consciousness. It includes positioning of the patient, passive and active movement of the limbs and joints, prevention of hand flexion and foot drop deformities. Attention must be paid to movement of joints, especially 'frozen' shoulder joint. Balance and standing can be restored gradually, starting with exercises for the lower limbs. Ultimately, walking is to be encouraged using sticks, frames and tripods, etc. During this period, the patient requires total care; nurses, physiotherapists and family members have to be extremely devoted.

The role of yoga in rehabilitation from stroke

Yoga clearly has something to offer in the sphere of rehabilitative medicine, and most promising research has been conducted in Czechoslovakia and Poland in this matter.[1] The most important single factor determining the relative importance of yoga in rehabilitation is the patient's own capacity and desire to regain the lost faculties. If they can understand the practices and if they possess the determination of will which is required to reactivate lost brain centres and overcome paralysis, muscular contraction, etc. associated with 'upper motor lesions' such as stroke, then the prognosis is excellent.

Of course, if the patient has lost all but the most fragmentary level of awareness, having to be fed, roused and guided like a child, then clearly yoga can do very little, because yoga depends first and foremost on the level of awareness with which the practices are performed. Practice with perseverance and determination will almost work miracles, but where the conscious connection with the victim is lacking, yoga cannot help very much, no matter how many people are wanting to assist.

Yogic practices for recovery from stroke

1. *Pawanmuktasana part 1 (anti-rheumatic series)*: These must be practised with full awareness and concentration, several

49

times a day. It is almost as if the patient has to consciously will the lost capacities back into the limbs. Paralysis is invariably on one side of the body, opposite to the side of the brain in which the stroke has occurred.

In the initial hours and days of a stroke, much of the brain tissues adjacent to the stroke area are in a state of shock, but in a few days the degree of incapacity and the level of consciousness can usually be assessed accurately. If alert and aware, the patient should then be instructed fully in the importance of the practices. It is up to him to bring back the functional deficit. That is the task he faces.

The patient should be actively trying to improve every moment of the day. He can begin by passive movements. If the left leg and arm are paralyzed, then he must commence by moving his left toes, ankle, fingers, wrist, knee and elbow passively, with the assistance of his right (good) hand. In this way, he has to gradually entice the function back. In the beginning, movements on the affected part of the body will be restricted and difficult, but the patient should persevere, keeping his full awareness on the practice, trying to feel and/or imagine the full range of movement on the affected side.

As improvement occurs, active movements should commence. Standing and walking should be struggled for and once he regains his feet, he has to cling to the upright posture at all costs, for all he is worth – levering himself up to his feet several times a day in the beginning. He should cast off despondency and dependency on others as early and as far as possible, doing everything possible for himself, no matter how long it takes. He must feed himself, comb his hair and use the bathroom by himself, even if the effort is enormous. There is no other way.

The period following a stroke is not meant to be a complete rest. That rest is not enough to revitalize the brain, to reforge the lost connections within the nervous system. Rest is most deep and rejuvenating when it comes at the point of exhaustion. The patient should thus rest in bouts, deeply, interspersed with periods of intense activity and effort. If he resorts to the rest program usually offered, he will never mobilize his lost capacities – he will only enjoy the tragic compulsory rest of an invalid, or worse, a vegetable, for the rest of his days.

2. *Yoga nidra and prana vidya*: Nor should the rest periods be given over to oblivion or drug induced slumber. In recovery from stroke, when mobilization of willpower is so important, the use of sedatives, sleeping tablets, tranquilizers, etc. is to be generally discouraged as these cloud the consciousness and fragment the will.

In yoga, we have to make another approach altogether. The patient has to practise yoga nidra whenever he slumbers. He has to constantly rotate his consciousness throughout the body parts, even though one whole half of his body will be insensible to him. Where he cannot feel a limb, he has to imagine its presence in his mind, create its image on the psychic plane. 'Right hand – left hand, right leg – left leg, right foot – left foot', like this he has to go on and on.

Then he has to create the mental image of his perfect body, not his paralyzed and stroke-ridden vehicle, but his perfect, golden, light body. This he has to visualize again and again by the power of his will and he has to direct energy, will force or prana right throughout that body, concentrating on those lost capacities he needs to regain. If it is the capacity to speak, then he must mobilize prana to the vocal cords; if it is the capacity to walk, then he must set himself a target and complete it first on the mental plane, step by step. Then he must perform that task within his physical body. This is the practice of prana vidya, healing oneself by awakening and directing the life force.

3. *Further asanas*: Utthanasana is the asana in which one rises from the squatting position to the upright stance, then descends again to the squat (knee-bent) position. This asana is most powerful in activating the proximal muscles of the legs, including the hamstring group at the back of the thighs, and the flexor group at the front of the thighs.

These are the two major groups of muscles involved when we stand up or sit down.

In stroke, the capacity to stand is most frequently lost, due to shock to the central connections of the motor nerves in the brain. This capacity to stand has to be consciously regained as soon as possible, and utthanasana becomes the struggle to rise from the chair or bed to the standing position and back again several times a day, using the arm of the chair, a wall or some other object for support. It should be practised after some motor function and sensation in the distal extremities (calves, feet, etc.) has been regained with the help of the pawanmuktasana series of exercises.

Simhagarjanasana is adopted where loss of the capacity to speak has occurred in the stroke. This may be due either to paralysis of the tongue and vocal cords (aphonia), or to damage higher in the brain causing a loss of the capacity to express thoughts in the form of language and words (aphasia). Simhargajanasana directs prana into the voice mechanism and restores lost or paralyzed vocal function. At a later stage, chanting and repetition aloud of specific mantras of precise meter, rhythm, rate and pronunciation (e.g. Durga Path) help to restore the more specific phonetic abilities and capacities involved in normal language.

Vajroli mudra (contraction of urethral sphincter muscles), ashwini mudra (contraction of anal sphincter) and moola bandha (perineum contraction) are useful in regaining conscious, voluntary control over bladder and bowel functions. Incontinence of urine and faeces frequently accompanies stroke; sometimes control never returns. By performing vajroli mudra and ashwini mudra, these two capacities can often be regained.

4. *Pranayama*: Nadi shodhana is the most important practice. As the efficiency of the cardiorespiratory cycle increases, the more advanced practices of kumbhaka and bandhas can be commenced very gradually, provided there is no hypertension, and then only with expert guidance and without any strain.

Kapalbhati pranayama, which relieves tension from the frontal region of the brain, is important in relieving cerebral venous thrombosis. It can be commenced in the convalescent phase when the acute condition is left behind and blood pressure is under control. Kapalbhati is contra-indicated in incomplete stroke and in intracerebral haemorrhage.

Bhramari, with its excellent healing effects, is also indicated.

5. *Meditation (japa yoga, antar mouna)*: Probably the most powerful and effective practices of all in restoring lost brain functions and in enhancing normal brain function are those in which we seek directly to become more aware, to wake up, to grow more conscious. Merely sitting quietly in one of the classical meditative postures has been shown to increase the cerebral blood flow. This is enhanced by the practice of mindfulness or witness awareness (antar mouna) or mantra repetition (japa, ajapa japa).

Cerebral Degeneration

What is the role of yoga in prevention of cerebral degeneration?

The process of cerebral degeneration in later life is well recognized. We accept that older people become physically slower, less alert mentally, have poorer eyesight and hearing, possess failing memories and reduced intellectual capacities. This is considered 'par for the course' or shall we call it 'normal pathology'? Senile dementia is the further fragmentation of consciousness which commonly occurs in the final stages of life. Here there is a disintegration of individual awareness, loss of contact with conventional realities, failure to recognize family members. It is accompanied by loss of awareness and control over bodily functions to such an extent that the helpless state of infancy comes clearly to mind. The two extremes of life are remarkably similar. This terminal descent into vegetal consciousness is also known as 'second childhood'. Frequently it develops only in the days or hours before physical death, but there are other cases in which it may continue for months or years.

Cerebral degeneration can be averted

According to both yoga and medical science, degeneration of the brain can be averted or at least decelerated.

In the past, pathologists have always taught that the degeneration of the brain in later life was due to a decrease in the number and capacity of the network of tiny arterioles and capillaries which supply the brain cells with oxygen. This was attributed to the process of arteriosclerotic degeneration of the arteries and arterioles in later life. Medical science therefore recommends a low fat diet, regular exercise, no smoking, and control of high blood pressure, as the most important steps in averting or, at least, slowing cerebral degeneration, and we are surely in agreement.

However, yoga has gone one step further in recognizing the fundamental cause of cerebral degeneration, and also in providing a set of psychophysiological practices which will avert and also alleviate cerebrovascular degeneration.

Recent study

In the past, pathologists have assumed that the ageing brain is progressively deprived of oxygen due to degenerative changes in the cerebral capillaries. However, a recent study reported in the *Journal of Gerontology*[1], which made a stereoscopic investigation of the capillaries in the cerebral cortex of 6 age groups ranging from 19 to 94 years, failed to find any evidence for this assumption. They found that capillary parameters such as diameter, volume, surface area and intercapillary distances per unit of cortical tissue in older patients over 75 years were similar to those in younger ones aged 19 to 44 years, and that the cerebral capillary network appears to be able to respond to changed metabolic conditions and alterations in blood pressure throughout life. This suggests that the actual aetiology of diminished brain function in later life may be a form of 'cerebral vasospasm' just as the aetiology of both coronary angina and myocardial infarction appears to be due to a mechanism of 'coronary vasospasm' (see IHD section).

Importance of blood supply

It now appears that the level of consciousness of an individual, which is reflected in the level of development of his brain, is determined by and reflected in the proportion of the cardiac output which continuously flows to the brain. An enhanced flow of blood throughout the brain appears to be the impetus to awaken the dormant human potentialities. As a result, the human higher capacities are systematically realized – memory, concentration, artistic appreciation, creativity, psychic capacities, etc. On the other hand, failure to maintain an adequate blood supply to the brain leads to cerebral degeneration, senile dementia and CVA.

Now, the underlying mechanism of cerebral degeneration is emerging. There is known to be a constant shunting of blood amongst the different major arterial beds of the body. This shunting is administered by the autonomic (sympathetic and parasympathetic) and voluntary nervous systems. In a sense, there is a constant competition between the different vascular beds for a limited supply of blood. This is borne out by everyday experience. After a meal, the visceral arterial bed is fully dilated to facilitate the digestive process. At this time we feel least inclined to concentrate, and most inclined to sleep because the cerebral capillaries are closed, and the blood supply to the brain is depleted.

Eventually we revive; however, it appears that if the digestive system is constantly overused and abused, the price we pay is some degree of cerebral degeneration. It is unlikely that a form of 'cerebral spasm' exists which reduces blood flow to the brain due to arterial spasm in response to stress levels. Neurotic, anxious and emotionally governed thought patterns induce 'coronary vasospasm' in the heart and precipitate the symptoms of IHD.

However, the brain's degenerative changes appear to occur in a simpler way. The cerebral vascular beds close down reflexly in response to the demand for extra blood in the other vascular beds. The brain, although the most important organ in our evolutionary journey, is thus paradoxically incapable of bolstering its own blood flow, except by the wilful practice of restraint, austerity, balance and harmony in the instinctual life.

56

Yoga enhances cerebral circulation

The practices of yoga have been shown to enhance cerebral blood flow in a unique way, thus systematically revealing the higher dormant potentialities of the brain. We can now appreciate the enormous value of the yoga practices from a physiological viewpoint in preventing cerebral degeneration and forging a higher, more conscious destiny for each of us. Four practices deserve special mention.

1. *Inverted asanas* such as sirshasana, sarvangasana and vipareeta karani mudra, induce a greater flow of blood into the head and brain. Sirshasana is traditionally known as the 'king of the asanas' and is highly valued for its rejuvenating influence upon the brain and pituitary gland. Some yogis remain in this posture for hours. Research studies have shown that cerebral blood flow and oxygen uptake increase markedly in the posture.[2,3]

2. *Meditative postures* including siddhasana and padmasana, have been shown to lead to a marked redistribution of blood flow, with increased cardiac output, coupled with declines in hepatic, renal and peripheral blood flow in the folded legs.[4] Increased cerebral and skin blood flows are hypothesized to account for the reshunted blood.

3. *Pranayama* has always been considered a most important discipline in the awakening and development of the higher brain. Studies have demonstrated that pranayama cannot be compared with simple breathing exercises such as deep breathing where oxygen intake is increased, but greater respiratory and cardiac work is also demanded. Pranayama is found to increase the supply of oxygen to the vital areas of the brain while simultaneously reducing the work load upon the heart. Pranayama represents an increased cardiorespiratory efficiency which leads to increased cerebral efficiency.

4. *Mudras and bandhas* are specific practices which exert precise physiological effects on the blood flow distribution patterns in the body, bringing about changes in the normally autonomic shunting of blood from one vascular

bed to another. Moola bandha and uddiyana bandha bring about a partial shutdown of the vascular beds of the pelvis and digestive system; this extra blood is made available to the beds of the brain and skin. Jalandhara bandha ensures that the cardiovascular dynamics of heart rate, blood pressure, etc., remain stable during this life-promoting shunting manoeuvre.

Yoga is life

The physiological influence of yoga practices in super-charging this effort to improve and elevate the function of the brain and become more conscious is clearly of paramount importance for our race. The best guarantee against cerebral degeneration is a combination of the moderate lifestyle recommended by pathologists (low fat vegetarian diet, adequate exercise, avoidance of smoking, etc.) supercharged by incorporating the yogic techniques which enhance cerebral blood flow.

Lowering the metabolic rate

There is evidence that cerebral degeneration can be pro-moted in another way as well, which may prove to be of great interest to the doctors, but, of course, must not be attempted by the heart patient under any conditions. Both yogic and scientific experience suggest that if the brain and central nervous system are gradually and systematically deprived of oxygen, they begin to operate in an altogether different way. Mental activity slows down and the body's metabolic rate drops, but death does not occur. It is possible to prolong human life by decades and even centuries in this manner, and even today, many yogis continue to practise this sadhana in isolation from the outside world.

This state of suspended physical and mental function is induced by specific techniques of pranayamic hypo-ventilation, in which the neurons of the brain gradually adapt themselves to a higher and higher concentration of carbon dioxide. The whole process can be induced by living in the same confined atmosphere for many days, weeks or even months. In respiratory physiology this is called 're-breathing'. The oxygen concentration of the gas diminishes day by day as it is used again and again, and simultaneously, the oxygen concentration of the blood also drops, while the concentration of carbon dioxide increases. But because the whole process is very gradual, there is no damage to the neurons. Instead, the cells of the brain become more and more efficient or, you can say, 'super-efficient'. They learn to squeeze oxygen from the bloodstream, just as the intestinal cells of a person who is slowly starving become highly efficient in extracting every nutrient from their meagre diet and even evolve new capacities to synthesize the missing vitamins. As the metabolic rate drops, the possibility of a much longer lifespan for the body and brain becomes a physiological reality. That is why yogis retire to a cave for years together, because it is the best place for rebreathing in a confined atmosphere.

Kaivalya kumbhaka
Evidence from the yogic texts and tradition indicates that systematic acclimatization of the brain to lower oxygen concentrations leads to a state of spontaneous suspension of the breath. This is kaivalya kumbhaka, a form of higher consciousness (samadhi) in which the ego is dissolved, while the brain commences to function in an enlightened natural way as a medium of universal consciousness. This is the pinnacle of human evolution and the ultimate outcome of yoga practice.

However, please note carefully that pranayamic hypo-ventilation can be extremely dangerous and even fatal, especially for anyone at risk from cardiovascular or cerebral disorders. It is a highly advanced stage of yogic sadhana and is only practised after years of intensive preparation under the direct guidance of a master. It is definitely not to be attempted or experimented with under any other circumstances.

The spectrum of brain function

If we consider the spectrum of brain efficiency, then the vascular accident lies at one extreme, representing the most severe and life threatening condition to which the human brain can succumb. This is characterized by clouding of consciousness, coma, unconsciousness and, frequently, death. Because of its overriding concern with severe pathology, medical science has as yet paid little attention to the other end of the spectrum of states of consciousness, failing to define accurately the 'normal' brain, and the 'normal' state of human consciousness. This gives medical science at present a very limited and incomplete picture of the total spectrum of human brain function, which actually extends from pathological conditions such as coma and stroke, in which the voltage of consciousness is extremely low, through the range of 'normal' or mundane consciousness. But the spectrum does not end there; yogic physiology extends far beyond the range of vision of medical science at the present time.

The normal brain is one tenth awake

In the yogic sciences, we do not consider that it is sufficient to be free of pathological stigmata of brain disease like coma, paralysis or amnesia. Absence of these symptoms is not a sufficient or scientific definition of the normal brain. Yogic understanding is that human conscious awareness is an evolving spectrum and that our present 'normal' condition is also a state of deficient brain function, even if our affliction is slightly less severe. Just because we are not in a dazed or comatose condition like the stroke victim, does not mean that we are absolutely awake and aware either.

We know from psychology that we are using only $1/10$ of the inherent capacities of our brain. This is a commonly accepted fact. Yet we never bother to draw the most obvious conclusions. It means that we are only $1/10$ conscious, $1/10$ awake, and $1/10$ aware. We are only $1/10$ in touch with our environment, $1/10$ in command of ourselves, $1/10$ of what we are biologically, physiologically and psychologically capable of being.

From our vantage point, we can see the stroke victim whose consciousness is dim and almost withdrawn. Perhaps he is only $1/20$ or 5% conscious, and we call it a tragedy. We see a formerly brilliant man or woman, perhaps one of our colleagues or teachers. His memory is failing, and he is becoming blind, and we call this a tragedy. We see older people, perhaps one of our own relatives, drifting into senility and dementia. We watch sadly as their personality changes, and again we say it is tragic, for he or she is $1/15$ or $7^1/_2$% conscious.

Yet we remain unaware of the greatest tragedy of all – that humanity as a whole, at the present stage and level of evolution, is only 10% conscious. We are all participating in the unfolding mystery of life while we remain $9/10$ asleep to what is really happening around us. We may be a professor, a doctor or a financial expert; we may have great eminence, position, wealth or power; yet, nevertheless, we are only $1/10$ of what we could be.

The vision of yoga

Yoga commences with the realization that we are not complete and perfect individuals in our present condition. Rather, there is something more to be known, realized or gained. We can surely become more aware of the dormant potentials and latent capacities of our brains. This is the prime task of yoga and its practices, which are designed to expand our consciousness beyond its present state of limitation.

In the yogic conception, the spectrum of consciousness continues through to higher states of awareness, character- ized by operation of brain capacities which are supernormal, superconscious or superefficient. These are the areas in which genius of one form or another becomes operational, be it musical, artistic, mathematical, financial, political or organizational. These are also areas in which psychic

61

capacities, or what researchers term 'paranormal abilities' – ESP, astral travel, distant healing, knowledge of past and future, and so on, manifest themselves.

The awakening of these higher functions of the human brain in some individuals illustrates clearly that our level of consciousness is by no means fixed, predetermined, or uniform, as we so commonly assume. The level we have reached now does not represent the ultimate product of human evolution. We represent an intermediate stage of development; we are not perfected beings. It is in this light that yoga views the operation of the human brain.

Awakening kundalini

The yogic conception of the 'normal' human brain is like a vast jewelled city in which there is a chronic power shortage. Only $^1/_{10}$ of the necessary current is available. As a result, the vast proportion of the city remains in darkness, even though the brain centres and the neuronal circuits, the powerhouses and the powerlines, are already established. In kundalini yoga, this city is known as sahasrara, the thousand-petalled lotus, at the crown of the head. The fullest flowering of this lotus represents the attainment of human perfection, the dawning of total conscious awareness which is called self-realization, moksha, kaivalya. That is the pinnacle of human evolution – 100% consciousness.

Kundalini yoga concerns itself directly with awakening the dormant unevolved potential. It is a science of transforming this limited brain into a greater, more evolved one. It is a very powerful yoga which must be practised directly under a guru's guidance. The power of energy of creation is unlimited. It is the primal impulse generating all life forms. This is kundalini.

In kundalini yoga, this energy is conducted progressively up through the various psychic centres (chakras) lying along the spinal column. Its source in the physical body is mooladhara chakra, the seat of the instinctive energies which fuel life on the animal plane of existence. We share

62

the instincts of reproduction and self-preservation with the animals. We possess a sex drive and a desire to eat, an instinctive seeking after pleasure and aversion for pain. These are the attributes which we inherit through animal life. These instincts, passions and desires operate through the various psychic centres – especially swadhisthana and manipura.

Mooladhara is conceptualized as a switch or powerhouse in the physical body. It is connected with the infinite source of primal energy which underlies the whole diverse spectrum of evolving life forms in the world. Mooladhara is located in the perineal floor in the male and in the posterior cervix in the female.

The task of kundalini yoga is to establish a high voltage powerline which will link this abundant powerhouse at the base of the spine with the dormant, darkened city of sahasrara at the top. This powerline is known as sushumna nadi, which flows within the centre of the spinal column.

All the practices of kundalini yoga are designed to forge this link, so that the evolutionary energy which is normally dissipated in the lower centres to satisfy the instincts, desires and passions, can be gradually redirected upwards and liberated into the brain.

Kundalini should not be considered as a fable, myth or fairy tale, nor should it be dismissed as unscientific. Kundalini is a biological and physiological event. It is not a religious topic to be preached from the pulpit, but a scientific phenomenon to be investigated in the laboratory. Even now the work of Dr Motoyama in Japan is revealing the psychophysiological reality of the nadis and chakras existing within our subtle anatomy.[5]

The practices to awaken kundalini are known as kriya yoga and are designed to transform a person into a super-being within a few years. This is the most powerful system of spiritual and cortical awakening known. Of course, it is unsuitable for stroke victims and can only be adopted by those who possess perfect health and a moderate lifestyle.

Purification of the body and training of the mind and the cardiorespiratory system are demanded for six months to two years before taking initiation into kriya yoga. Asana, pranayama and shatkriya must be perfected. Nevertheless, it is from these practices, designed to awaken super-consciousness within 'normal' people, that we can draw a set of preliminary practices which will help victims of cerebral degeneration regain their lost physical capacities and mental functions.

Question 8

Peripheral Vascular Disease of the Lower Extremities

Is yogic management effective in cases of peripheral vascular disease in the lower extremities, including intermittent claudication, gangrene, etc.?

Peripheral vascular disease in the legs is a major problem occurring in middle and later life. Although this disease is rarely a cause of death, it is nevertheless a cause of much morbidity and suffering. Its management poses a difficult surgical problem.

In general, peripheral vascular disease in the legs can be divided into two distinct categories:
1. Disturbances of arterial circulation which are a part of generalized arteriosclerotic syndrome.
2. Disturbances of venous return from the legs which are unrelated to arteriosclerosis.

DISTURBANCES OF ARTERIAL CIRCULATION

Arterial blood enters the legs via the iliac arteries, which are the two terminal branches of the abdominal aorta. Peripheral arterial disease is the term applied to the process of arteriosclerotic vascular degeneration in the arteries and arterioles of the legs, resulting in ischaemia of the muscles and tissues of either one or both legs. This occurs as a part of the more general arteriosclerotic process. It usually accompanies symptoms of arteriosclerosis elsewhere in the

65

arterial network, especially in the coronary and cerebral vascular beds.

Predisposing factors

In peripheral arterial disease predisposing factors include: lack of exercise, high fat diet, smoking, stress, hypertension and diabetes.

Symptoms

Symptoms of peripheral arterial disease are variable. Mild degrees of arterial deficiency may manifest as coldness or a tingling of the feet. This may be accompanied by cramps and spasms of the calf and foot muscles, occurring especially at night.

More severe degrees of arterial insufficiency will give rise to intermittent claudication, which refers to pains arising in the leg muscles during exercise. These are relieved by rest, in the same way that coronary angina is relieved by rest. In fact, coronary angina and intermittent claudication arise by the same vascular mechanism (muscular ischaemia) operating in different parts of the body, and a patient of generalized arteriosclerosis frequently experiences both symptoms simultaneously upon exertion and exercise.

Gangrene is a symptom of severe peripheral vascular disease. This is the decay (necrosis) of a segment of the leg, foot or toes due to oxygen starvation. It occurs following sudden obstruction of the blood supply caused by spasm of the arteries of the thighs due to overexcitation of their sympathetic nerves. Another possible cause is the formation of a blood clot within the artery (thromboembolism). It may also occur as a complication of severe vascular degeneration in long-standing, uncontrolled diabetes.

Where sudden obstruction occurs higher up in one of the major arteries of the leg, there is the risk of gangrene developing in the whole limb. This is a surgical emergency, which appears as a cold pale limb in which arterial pulses are absent. Unless the obstruction can be rapidly diagnosed (often utilizing x-ray angiography) and relieved by arterial surgery, irreversible tissue degeneration and death of the limb is inevitable, and amputation is performed. This is the usual cause for lower limb amputation, apart from accident or injury.

The role of yoga in peripheral arterial disease

A large number of clinical studies have revealed that yoga asanas have a decisive role to play in both central and peripheral vascular degeneration. One Indian study of eight major yogasanas revealed that these induced an increase in blood flow to the extremities, while simultaneously lowering the heart and respiratory rates.[1] This means increased circulatory efficiency with reduced cardiac strain, suggesting that yogasanas, in contradiction to other systems of exercise, induce coronary relaxation and exert an overall rejuvenating influence in the degenerated arteriosclerotic cardiovascular system by inducing a redistribution of blood flow amongst the major arterial beds of the body.

Another American study of yogic relaxation and simple meditation has produced similar findings. Researchers, using blood cells labelled with radioactive isotopes, found that yogic relaxation induces a lowering of cardiac output, a decreased blood flow in the renal and hepatic (liver) arterial beds and increased blood flow to the brain, skin and extremities.[2]

This suggests that the degenerative patterns of coronary, cerebral and peripheral arterial disease occur due to a chronic deficiency of oxygen supply to those capillary beds. This occurs because the total blood volume of about 4.8 litres is continually shunted away from these vital beds and into the arterial beds of the digestive, excretory and reproductive systems, in response to our habitual and often excessive demands upon these systems. Physiologically, it appears that we starve our brain, heart and peripheral vessels in order to keep supplying blood to our undisciplined and overworked digestive, metabolic and excretory systems.

67

In order to bring about a reshunting of blood into the vital coronary, cerebral and peripheral beds, a yogic lifestyle incorporating asana, pranayama, meditation and relaxation is needed. In response to this, habits change and the health improves. As meditation and asanas become a part of our daily routine, like cleaning the teeth and tongue every morning, there is an automatic reshunting of blood into those arterial beds where chronic oxygen lack or vasospasm is the problem, and away from those beds where excessive usage and organ depletion are the usual causes of disease (e.g. digestive disorders, diabetes and genito-urinary diseases).

This concept of the automatic shunting of a limited volume of blood between the different major vascular beds of the body (coronary, cerebral, digestive, renal and peripheral) by the voluntary and autonomic nervous systems in response to our physiological and metabolic demands and lifestyle habits, is revolutionary. The concept of deficient blood flow in an artery as the fundamental cause of sclerotic degeneration of that artery itself is also revolutionary.

In order to preserve our cerebral, coronary and peripheral vascular beds from decay, we must follow a lifestyle which includes those techniques which have been shown to induce a shunting of blood away from renal and hepatic beds and into the cerebral, coronary and peripheral beds. That is the yogic life, based on meditation, pranayama, asana and relaxation. These are the techniques which bestow life and allay death. They are the secrets of rejuvenation and the nectar of immortality. Yoga is the bestower of life.

Blood coagulation studies

One of the major precipitating factors in vascular degeneration is a high level of cholesterol and fats (lipids) in the blood. This accompanies an abnormally high level of metabolic activity of the liver and consumption of a diet rich in saturated fats. Such a heavy, fatty diet demands that the digestive processes be continually operational and requires a high and prolonged shunting of blood into the visceral arterial beds. This is probably one of the major factors leading to cerebrovascular, cardiovascular and peripheral vascular degeneration because of long-term deprivation of oxygen to these arterial beds. Furthermore, the blood itself is found to be more turbid and viscous, and extra work is demanded of the heart in order to continually pump this thicker blood throughout the body, just as it is more difficult to pump a dense fluid which is like milk than one like water.

In addition, the blood is found to have a higher tendency to clot, because the specific factors and enzymes responsible for the blood clotting mechanism are synthesized in higher quantities in an overactive liver. Thrombus (clot) formation in the arteries and its subsequent liberation into the bloodstream as an embolus to lodge elsewhere in the arterial tree is one of the major causes of peripheral vascular obstruction and CVA.

A recent study has come to the conclusion that yoga practices induce a state of hypocoagulability, rendering the blood less prone to the dangers of clot formation and thromboembolism.[3] Raised fibrinolytic (clot breakdown) activity and decreased platelet stickiness, reflecting reduced clumping and adherence of the circulating red blood cells, were also recorded.

Yoga program in peripheral arterial disease

1. *Asana*: Pawanmuktasana 1 and 2, surya namaskara, paschimottanasana, akarna dhanurasana, vajrasana, shashankasana, supta vajrasana, dhanurasana, shalabhasana, padmasana, yoga mudra, matsyasana, trikonasana, sarvangasana/vipareeta karani mudra, shavasana/yoga nidra relaxation.
2. *Pranayama*: Nadi shodhana, agnisar kriya.
3. *Bandhas*: Uddiyana bandha, moola bandha.
4. *Meditation*: Yoga nidra, ajapa japa.

DISTURBANCES OF VENOUS RETURN FROM THE LEGS

This syndrome includes varicose veins, varicose ulcers, oedematous swelling of the legs and feet, superficial and deep venous thrombosis, etc. Here there is a pooling of venous blood and lymphatic fluid in the legs.

Varicose veins

Veins in the legs which have lost their valvular competence are known as varicose veins. These are an occupational hazard for those who must stand still in one position for long periods, e.g. policemen. Venous return is facilitated by the 'muscle pump' created by the rhythmic contraction and relaxation of the leg muscles in walking. By standing motionless this pump, which has been called 'the second heart', is rendered inoperative, and movement of the column of blood in the venous system from the feet up to the heart becomes sluggish. Under the pressure of this column of blood, some of the internal (one-way) flow valves within the veins give way and an unsightly, dependent varicose vein gradually develops at that site.

Varicose veins also frequently arise during pregnancy, due to obstruction to venous return by the enlarging uterus, and also occur secondary to traumatic injury or accident to the veins.

Varicose veins give rise to pain, tiredness and heaviness in the legs, especially by the end of the day. Often the main complaint is an aesthetic one.

Venous ulcers

Venous ulcers (also known as varicose ulcers or dependent ulcers) are a frequent complication of poor venous return in the limbs. Because of pooling of extra cellular fluid (lymph), even the slightest injury proves difficult to heal. Slight wounds frequently degenerate into major ulcers, especially on the shins, and the surrounding area becomes

70

deeply pigmented due to the breakdown of blood pooled in the tissues. The surrounding skin becomes leathery and full of fluid. A low grade, chronic inflammatory reaction usually develops (cellulitis) and pitting edema is present.

Surgical/medical management of varicose veins and ulcers
The first principle in management is to promote venous return from the legs to the heart. In medicine this is achieved by elevating the patient's legs in bed, so that no dependent venous blood collects while sleeping. During the day, elastic bandages which serve as an auxiliary muscle pump and prevent venous distension are usually applied. Resting with the legs elevated, and walking rather than standing still are also advised.

Healing of varicose ulcers is a tedious and time-consuming affair. Healing is found to proceed rapidly if the dependent oedema of the tissues can be reduced. These ulcers usually develop out of neglect, and their healing demands daily attention, meticulous dressing and care, often for months. In severe cases skin grafting may be considered necessary.

Varicose veins which are unsightly or troublesome frequently come to surgery, where they are stripped, ligated or injected with adherent (sclerosing) substances. Venous drainage of the area is then maintained by a more competent collateral route. Immediate relief is gained, but this is often only temporary, as sclerosed veins have a tendency to reappear, while surgical stripping and obliteration of one major vein frequently precipitates varicose changes in another nearby vein.

Yogic management of varicose veins and ulcers
Specific yoga asanas often prove very effective in relieving and even curing varicose veins and ulcers, especially in the early stages of development. Asanas are especially beneficial in recovery after childbirth, when valvular competence lost in pregnancy can often be regained. These asanas also

71

prove useful in recovery from valvular injury after traumatic accidents. Those who suffer from varicose veins are advised to practise yoga asanas on a daily basis for a trial period of at least two months. If no improvement in the condition occurs, then surgical procedures may be indicated.

The asanas are prescribed in groups according to their specific effects.

1. Asanas to promote venous drainage and bring relief from leg heaviness, pain and tiredness. These should be practised several times each day for several minutes: vipareeta karani mudra, sarvangasana (in the final position, rhythmic contraction/relaxation of calf and thigh muscles should be performed), leg cycling and leg circling, pawanmuktasana for feet, legs and hips.

2. Asanas to help restore valvular competence: surya namaskara, parvatasana, paschimottanasana, halasana, tadasana, pada hastasana, balancing asanas, garudasana, gomukhasana.

3. Asanas to regulate blood supply in the lower half of the body: padmasana, siddhasana, yoga mudra, matsyasana, vajrasana, shashankasana, supta vajrasana.

4. Practices to enhance venous return to the heart by generating a negative intra-abdominal pressure which helps to 'suck' blood from the legs back into the right side of the heart: naukasana, ardha shalabhasana, shalabhasana, ujjayi pranayama, uddiyana bandha.

Question 9

Vasospastic Diseases of the Microcirculation

(Raynaud's Disease)

What is the yogic management of vasospastic diseases of the microcirculation (Raynaud's disease)?

Raynaud's phenomenon is a disturbance of the peripheral blood vessels, consisting of spasmodic contraction of the digital arteries of the fingers and/or toes, which is precipitated by cold or emotion. Primary Raynaud's phenomenon usually commences in childhood and is no more than a hypersensitive or exaggerated physiological response to cold. It is also called 'chilblains' and is far more common in cold countries and climates.

Secondary Raynaud's phenomenon refers to a similar condition which occurs due to obliterative arterial disease, pressure from an accessory cervical rib, or as an employment hazard in certain occupations in which the arms and hands are exposed to high frequency vibrations from pneumatic drills, polishing tools, etc. The changes are confined to the digits, and in severe cases, the disorder may lead to secondary changes in the arterioles, ischaemic changes in the skin of the digits and nails, superficial necrosis and eventually gangrene.

Pathology

The cause of this disorder appears to be an increased vasomotor tone due to an excessive level of sympathetic control over the peripheral arteries. In other cases the sensory nerves of the arteries appear to be excessively sensitive to cold, responding with an exaggerated 'spastic' reaction.

No pathological changes are observed in the early stages, which could be termed 'digital vasospasm'. At a later stage, obliteration, blockage and thrombosis of the terminal arteries usually occurs, resulting in prolonged tissue ischaemia and finally gangrene.

Signs and symptoms

The symptoms usually occur bilaterally, and fingers are more frequently affected than toes. Parastesia, numbness, tingling and burning are more prominent than pain. Sensitivity to cold may be extreme. Colour changes in the fingers or toes occur in three phases: pallor, cyanosis and redness. If the digit is bloodless, it will be pale; if blood flow is sluggish, excessive deoxygenation renders it blue (cyanosis); redness occurs as a reaction or rebound phenomenon due to excessive vasodilation and reactive hyperaemia which may follow spasm.

Medical and surgical management

Medical and surgical management of this phenomenon are disappointing. Vasodilator drugs usually prove ineffective. Protection from cold is the most important step. Smoking is believed to be a major contributing factor and must be given up. In severe cases, the surgical disconnection of the sympathetic nerve supply to the limb to remove the excessive vasomotor tone and relieve vasospasm may be performed, but results of this procedure are also disappointing. This is still a poorly understood and managed disorder.

Yogic management of Raynaud's disease

There is a great deal of evidence to suggest that yoga will emerge as the treatment of choice for this disease in the near future. The disease is characterized by excessive activity in the sympathetic nerves responsible for vascular reactivity

74

of the digital arteries. These nerves regulate the flow of blood entering the fingers or toes. In particular, there is a loss of the capacity for thermoregulation, due to a loss of autonomic balance in the arteries of the skin.

Several important studies have clearly illustrated that yoga practices increase peripheral blood flow, relax muscular tone and reduce sympathetic nervous activity in the body[1,2] while other studies have shown that the galvanic skin conductance response (GSR) was significantly decreased after 6 months of yogic relaxation and meditation practices.[3] Decreased GSR is recognized as a measure of decreased sympathetic nervous activity and increased stress resistance.[4] The effectiveness of yogic relaxation as a means of thermo-regulation has been verified in many further studies.[5,6,7] This is essentially a means of 'willing oneself warm'. One of the most significant demonstrations of this capacity occurred in 1977 at the Menninger Foundation in Kansas (USA) when an Indian yogi, Swami Rama, was able to demonstrate and maintain a temperature difference of 10 degrees between the dorsal and palmar surfaces of his hands.[8]

Another research group made a direct clinical study of the effectiveness of relaxation in treating thirty female sufferers from Raynaud's disease.[9] All the patients revealed the ability to maintain digital skin temperature in the presence of a cold stress challenge, and reported significant reductions in both frequency and intensity of vasospasmodic attacks. In this study the addition of skin temperature biofeedback to the yoga nidra practice did not provide additional clinical benefit.

Yoga practices for peripheral vasospasm
1. *Pawanmuktasana part 1*, which promotes relaxation and blood flow into the peripheral circulation in the extremities, is the most important asana series.
2. *Surya namaskara* promotes circulation of body fluids and stimulates peripheral circulation in the extremities.

3. *Nadi shodhana pranayama* balances the sympathetic and parasympathetic nervous system, restoring autonomic control and vascular stability.
4. *Yoga nidra*, emphasizing rotation of consciousness and creation of the experience of heat in the body, especially in the hands and feet, forms the most effective single practice for the cure of Raynaud's disease. The patient learns to master the wayward autonomic response consciously.

Question 10

Techniques for Arteriosclerotic Degenerative Diseases

Which yogic techniques are most appropriate for arterio-sclerotic degenerative diseases?

Yoga nidra

Yoga nidra is one of the most important practices in the yogic management of ischaemic heart disease (IHD), cerebral vascular degeneration (CVD) and hypertension (H/T). Its application has already been fully outlined in the following sections:
- Hypertension (Datey's study)
- Ischaemic heart disease
- Heart attack (nada yoga and the coronary posture)
- Cerebrovascular disease (prana vidya)
- Raynaud's disease (the experience of heat)

Pranayama

In managing the coronary situation we make no effort to teach pranayama in the conventional way, but we definitely lead the patient to the breath as a vehicle of relaxation. We ensure that there is never any question of straining, withholding or resisting the breath. That is completely contraindicated. Instead, the patient learns to befriend the spontaneous inflowing and outflowing breath, making no conscious effort to control it in any way. He only witnesses it effortlessly.

Nadi shodhana (with anuloma viloma) is the single most important pranayama discussed in sections on:
- Coronary vasospasm
- Arrhythmias (the coronary pranayama, a combination of nadi shodhana and ujjayi)
- Cerebrovascular disease
- Raynaud's disease

Bhramari pranayama is useful in cardiac and cerebro-vascular recovery, and also in diseases characterized by a high level of cerebral tension including epilepsy and asthma. It is both a pranayama and one of the practices of nada yoga. The process is very subtle and must be learned correctly. It is one of internal absorption into the humming sound. It is practised in a sitting position.

In the texts of yoga, the heart centre is termed 'the centre of unstruck sound', and also 'the cave of bees'. In bhramari the humming sound of the bees is produced and traced towards its source. This induces deep mental and emotional relaxation. The sound is produced with gentle exhalation. It must take place effortlessly, without undue strain to prolong the vibration or to change its pitch or loudness. It should only be spontaneous, and it can be very soft. It is essentially an internal sound, and when the ears are blocked with the fingers, the patient is instructed to follow the inner vibration and discover its source.

Kapalbhati pranayama involves a forced exhalation. It is contraindicated in the case of coronary disorders including hypertension, but is useful in cases of cerebrovascular degeneration due to venous thrombosis of the cerebral sinuses. Kapalbhati exerts a decompressing effect upon the brain, especially the frontal lobes.

Abdominal respiration is initially practised from shav-asana. Here, the rise and fall of the navel becomes the object of awareness. It is especially useful in providing a central focus of awareness or being in the body for those whose breath is characteristically rapid and shallow, accompanied by a high level of anxiety (anxiety neurosis) and worry. This practice grounds the awareness in the navel, establishing contact between the upward movement of prana from diaphragm to throat, and the downward movement of apana from navel to perineum. It defuses many imaginary fears and illusions which disrupt the cardiorespiratory ratios and precipitate cardiac instability.

In the coronary situation, we develop abdominal awareness in the patient gradually, as a matter of course. He learns to choose the navel as his best vantage point, as it rises and falls spontaneously with the breathing cycle.

Abdominal breath awareness is found to exert a profound physiological influence. It automatically alters the filling pattern of the lobes of the lungs, and also conserves and generates energy. Respiration becomes more relaxed and efficient. At the same time the heart rate slows, but without compromising the cardiorespiratory efficiency, which actually increases.

Abdominal respiration is a vital initiation for anxious, fearful cardiac patients, who are often rapid, shallow breathers, confining the breath to the upper chest cavity in parallel with their cardiac tension. There is a failure of diaphragmatic descent and the patient remains unaware of the connection between his breath and his conscious experiences of pain, fear, etc. This practice changes the focus of awareness, untying the psychophysiological knot in the heart region, which has been tightening for many anxious years.

Ujjayi pranayama is very important in management of both hypertension and cardiac diseases. It is a powerful method to rest and strengthen the heart and its actions. When combined with mantra repetition and ascent and descent of awareness in the frontal psychic passage between navel and throat (ajapa japa) it becomes a most powerful system of meditation which leads to transcendence of the personal emotional metabolism associated with the lower psychic centres, and liberation of the emotional energy upon the transcendental plane (akasha) symbolized by the

79

throat centre (vishuddhi). This transformation of emotional awareness is symbolized by the untying of Vishnu granthi – the psychic knot or blockage centred in the heart.

In the 'coronary pranayama', ujjayi is initially practised in shavasana, without khechari mudra. It can be combined with anuloma viloma.

Sheetali and seetkari are two cooling pranayamas which are employed in the management of hypertension. They cool the column of inhaled air, and this coolness is conducted to the gas exchange areas and thence into the bloodstream. These pranayamas cool the blood and cool down a 'hot head' – the build–up of mental tension due to unexpressed frustration, passion and rage which creates hypertension.

Meditation

Meditation (dhyana yoga) is a fundamental component of yogic life. Evolution of personal awareness through meditation is pursued directly by four separate systems of meditation which are suited to the needs and requirements of the individual. They are of graded difficulty and have slightly different indications, even though each is designed to evolve the awareness directly. The four systems used most frequently in cardiovascular disease are yoga nidra, ajapa japa, antar mouna and kriya yoga.

Yoga nidra is used in the therapeutic situation to relieve anxiety, induce relaxation and hasten recovery and rehabilitation. It is especially important in the acute coronary situation. Its application has already been outlined in previous sections.

Ajapa japa is used in coronary rehabilitation in conjunction with ujjayi pranayama as a part of the 'coronary pranayama'. In this practice, awareness of the mantra and the movement of the psychic breath in the frontal psychic passage between the navel and throat is developed. This is especially prescribed in disorders where emotional blockages are prominent. Its normalizing influence upon cardiac metabolism is profound, as it channels emotions away from objects of personal obsession and towards the transcendental plane. It is a fundamental practice for prevention of cardiovascular degeneration, and is one of the most important preparatory practices for kriya yoga. Mantra initiation from the guru or spiritual preceptor should precede the practice, or a general mantra such as Soham, Om or Gayatri may be used.

Antar mouna (inner silence) is the tantric system of meditation which is based on establishing 'witness awareness'. The vipassana meditation followed by Dr K.N. Udupa of Benares Hindu University is a form of 'mindfulness meditation' used in Hinayana Buddhism. It is similar to antar mouna.[1]

Antar mouna is a stepwise process of inducing sense withdrawal (pratyahara) and then mental concentration (dharana and dhyana). It commences with witness awareness of the outside sounds and physical sensations and culminates with the dissolution of all mental activity. That is the experience of the merging of subjective and objective awareness as the mind itself dissolves into the universal consciousness.

Antar mouna is practised not only for spiritual enlightenment, but also for health and mental wellbeing. It is an important practice for prevention of cardiovascular degeneration. It is a slightly more advanced technique and is well suited for intellectually querulous people.

Kriya yoga is the most powerful system of accelerating the personal evolution and developing the awareness. It is a complete and all-embracing sadhana which involves 20 specific kriyas or practices in a fixed sequence. All the practices of yoga are actually preparations for this system of yoga. Each kriya is a combination of asana, pranayama, mudra, bandha and dhyana. Kriya yoga demands good health and adequate preparation. The body must be pure and the mind must be stable at the outset. It is an excellent preventive sadhana for all forms of degenerative disease, but has little place in the conventional therapeutic sense. However, a few simplified kriyas are often adapted to specific disease conditions – for example, 'the coronary posture' (utthanpadasana, Rama karani mudra) is a simplified version of the first kriya, vipareeta karani mudra.

Asana

Doctors are very timorous about prescribing postures for cardiac patients, but in yogic management asanas have a very important part to play both in restoration and preservation of cardiac functions. Asanas must be prescribed in a scientific way, much as you prescribe drugs and medicines. Each asana and pranayama has specific indications and contraindications.

At the outset, when cardiac reserve is very poor, shavasana and the 'coronary posture' (a variation of utthanpadasana), which increase the cardiac output while resting the heart, are the only recommended postures. Then, as recovery continues, cardiac rehabilitation can proceed according to the needs of the individual patient.

No two patients are the same, so no one should compete with anyone else. Initiation into yoga should be effortless, natural and spontaneous. Each should go on at his own rate with a skilled guide to ensure that the fundamental principles are learned; then he can continue with his own daily practice. Half an hour or 45 minutes each morning is sufficient, followed by pranayama and yoga nidra. Yoga nidra should be repeated in the afternoon for 20 to 30 minutes as well. Cardiac reserve increases rapidly after the initial few weeks of recovery and stabilization, and very few restrictions need be applied. Most of the major asanas can be gradually adopted, but there should be no strain, and adequate relaxation must be included after each posture.

We have found that the pawanmuktasana part 1 series of anti-rheumatic exercises provides the best introduction, preparing the body and mind gradually for major asanas later on. Then we introduce the pawanmuktasana part 2 series of digestive promotive exercises such as supta pawanmuktasana (leg lock), pada sanchalanasana (leg cycling), chakra padasana (leg rotation), jhulana lurhakanasana (rocking and rolling). The next step is surya namaskara, performed slowly and rhythmically two or three times, followed by relaxation in shavasana. This activates the heart and circulation and should begin every asana session.

Major asanas should begin with vajrasana and its variations – marjari-asana, shashankasana, shashank bhujangasana and ushtrasana. Then, padmasana, yoga mudra, matsyasana, dhanurasana, shalabhasana, bhujangasana, paschimottanasana and ardha matsyendrasana. There are very few restrictions necessary. However, the inverted asanas (vipareeta karani asana, sarvangasana, halasana) should be avoided until all signs of subnormal cardiac function have disappeared, and until blood pressure is well under control and stable, without medication. Then vipareeta karani can be commenced only for half a minute in the beginning.

Meditative asanas are important in prevention of cardiovascular degeneration, because they induce an automatic shunting of blood to the arterial beds of the brain and skin, imposing no added strain on the heart.

Siddhasana exerts a powerful stabilizing influence upon the hormonal and reproductive metabolism in the male, stabilizing cardiac behaviour and fluctuating blood pressure levels in the early years when emotional and sexual drives and passions are likely to be unruly. At that time, siddhasana is found to rectify problems such as excessive nocturnal emission. If followed throughout life, it stabilizes sudden fluctuations in blood pressure which precipitate arterial degeneration, hypertension and cardiac demise later in life. It is recommended by Dr Christian Barnard to stabilize cardiac function.[2] The recent demonstration of receptors for testosterone in the walls of the heart's chambers offers a physiological explanation for this destructive influence on the heart (refer to the discussion of testosterone in Question 4: Heart Disease).

YOGA PROGRAMS

For cardiac convalescence and initial rehabilitation

1. *Asana*: Shavasana, coronary posture (a variation of utthanpadasana); pawanmuktasana part 1 practices for hands, feet, wrists and ankles can be done lying in bed.
2. *Pranayama*: Abdominal breathing with counting of the breath. The 'coronary pranayama' (combination of anuloma viloma and ujjayi); bhramari.
3. *Mudra*: Hridaya mudra.
4. *Relaxation*: Yoga nidra, nada yoga.

For further rehabilitation (when condition has fully stabilized)

1. *Asana*: Pawanmuktasana part 1, shavasana, vajrasana, shashankasana, shashank-bhujangasana, marjariasana, hasta utthanasana, akarna dhanurasana, eka pada pranamasana, bhujangasana, saral dhanurasana, paschimottanasana, ardha shalabhasana, yoga mudra, matsyasana.
2. *Pranayama*: Abdominal respiration, ujjayi, nadi shodhana, mild bhastrika, sheetali/seetkari.
3. *Relaxation*: Yoga nidra.
4. *Meditation*: Ajapa japa, antar mouna.
5. *Hatha yoga*: Neti kriya.

For prevention of cardiovascular degeneration

1. *Asana*: Surya namaskara, pawanmuktasana part 3 series, paschimottanasana, vajrasana, shashankasana, supta vajrasana, shashank-bhujangasana, padmasana, yoga mudra, matsyasana, ardha matsyendrasana, trikonasana, vipareeta karani mudra, sarvangasana, halasana.
2. *Pranayama*: Nadi shodhana with maha bandha, bhastrika, ujjayi, agnisar kriya.
3. *Relaxation*: Neti kriya. Shankhaprakshalana under guidance and taking into account all precautions.
4. *Meditation*: Ajapa japa, antar mouna, kriya yoga.

Question 11

Respiratory Diseases

What are the particular postures and respiratory rhythms used for asthma, chronic bronchitis and emphysema? Have their effects on respiratory functions been checked?

The different types of obstructive airways diseases have been treated by yoga for millennia. In our own ashrams in India and abroad, we have successfully treated literally thousands of respiratory sufferers over the past decade. In recent years, clinical trials have validated our own experiences and we have undertaken and published the results of an Asthma Camp conducted at our Raipur ashram in conjunction with J.N.M. Medical College, Raipur.[1]

Asthma

Asthma is an illness where the sufferer has recurrent episodes of constriction of the breathing passages (bronchi) of the lungs. As a result, he experiences severe attacks of difficulty in breathing. In asthma, the major obstruction is with the expiratory part of the breathing cycle. The lungs become hyperinflated with air and it is very difficult for the asthmatic to initiate the normal expiratory or relaxing phase of the cycle. Instead, he tries to push the air out against the increased resistance of the spasmed airways, and this effort further worsens the situation.

In health, and between asthma attacks, the ratio of inhalation/exhalation approaches 1:2, but in acute asthma, expiration may be greatly extended. Expiration is long, wheezy, tiring and ineffectual, and may approach 1:4 or more. The struggle for oxygen may continue for hours or even days, until finally exhaustion and sleep supervene. At the moment when the patient is too tired to struggle and has given up all efforts, the breath suddenly reverts to a normal relaxed rhythm spontaneously of its own accord.

In yoga therapy we induce the premature termination of the attack by postures which both encourage and demand deep and relaxed respiration from the chest and abdomen as a matter of course. These cause a natural and spontaneous breathing cycle to be readopted. This must be done in such a way that no conscious effort is required to achieve it, because asthma is a peculiar disease in which all self-motivated efforts only worsen the situation. The only useful effort the asthmatic can make is the effort to surrender.

Yogic practices for asthma

The major yogic practices in the treatment of asthma are the group of hatha yoga shatkarmas, especially kunjal kriya (swallowing warm, salty water and regurgitating it), neti kriya (pouring warm water through the alternate nostrils) and vastra dhauti (swallowing a specially prepared cloth strip and then pulling it out again to stimulate the oesophagus). In addition, poorna shankhaprakshalana, or its shorter form, laghoo shankhaprakshalana, are performed whenever constipation is complicating the problem.

Asanas are an important component of yogic management of asthma. Our program includes surya namaskara as a matter of course to all asthmatics, as it both demands and creates an acceptable breathing rhythm. It is not only a dynamic series, but also an involuntary form of pranayama. Two or three rounds should be performed slowly in the beginning, followed by complete rest in shavasana. We have found a few particular asanas which exert a profound influence upon the asthmatic respiratory cycle. We are making attempts to evaluate these changes in respiratory

86

function using spirometry and other lung function tests, and of course much work still lies ahead of us.

The asanas commence with vajrasana. Resting in this posture leads automatically to a deeper abdominal respiration pattern. Then shashankasana is performed, which exerts an influence upon the adrenal glands, modulating the secretion of steroid hormones from the adrenal cortex into the bloodstream and controlling the liberation of noradrenalin from the adrenal medulla. This posture leads to an automatic change in the filling patterns of the lobes of the lungs, by deepening the depth of respiration and descent of the diaphragm. The patient rests in the forward position, maintaining awareness of the abdominal respiration. After some time he reverts to vajrasana, then performs the head down posture once again. This practice is sufficient to control an asthma attack.

In addition to shashankasana, we introduce marjari-asana, ushtrasana and supta vajrasana for variation. All act to harmonize the adrenal glandular secretions and induce a deeper, more relaxed abdominal respiration pattern, and each is performed from vajrasana.

Pranamasana is an important inverted asana performed from vajrasana. Here, the top of the head is in contact with the floor and the buttocks are raised in order to fully stretch the cervical and first few thoracic vertebrae. This decompresses the cervical sympathetic ganglia responsible for spasm of the bronchi and also promotes drainage of thick mucous secretions out of the bronchial tree. It bestows great relief in asthma. Sarvangasana (shoulder stand) may also be adopted, as it induces similar results.

The backward bending asanas decompress the hunched forward thoracic spine of an asthma sufferer, liberating pent up nervous energy in the cervical and thoracic sympathetic nerves and ganglia and moving the breath in the direction of spontaneous release and relaxation. These include shashank bhujangasana, dhanurasana, chakrasana and bhujangasana.

87

Utthita lolasana is a dynamic standing asana in which the upper body drops forward from the waist as the lungs are emptied. This has the effect of releasing the expiratory spasm and increasing the forced expiratory volume (FEV) in an asthmatic attack.

Pranayama is practised in conjunction with asana in the management of asthma. Especially in the acute attack, abdominal respiration and ujjayi are a basic part of the asana program. Pranayama leads to greater control of the respiratory cycle and by practising nadi shodhana or bhastrika at the time of onset of asthmatic attack, autonomic balance can usually be restored and the attack alleviated.

Yoga nidra practised in shavasana and ajapa japa and antar mouna in siddhasana or padmasana are essential for recognizing and eliminating the root cause of asthma in the subconscious mind.

CLINICAL RESEARCH STUDIES

1. The asthma study in Raipur ashram

Our study of the Asthma Camp held at Raipur Yogashram revealed considerable improvements in respiratory function in most of the participants. The trial was conducted by Dr G.B. Gupta, Professor G.C. Sepaha and a team of researchers from Raipur Medical College. Two thirds (18) of the 27 asthmatic patients studied showed improvement in their condition after learning and practising yoga.

Respiratory functions were tested with a spirometer before, during and after the camp. Spirometer readings, which measure the degree of freedom of breathing, showed that 62.5% of patients had definite relaxation and dilation of the bronchial tubes, and experienced greater freedom of breath due to yoga.

2. Meditation and asthma

Medical science attributes asthma to a combination of psychological, allergic and hereditary factors. Many asthmatics seem to possess unusually difficult, hyper-sensitive personalities.

Meditation is found useful in asthma, helping the sufferer to recognize the subconscious mechanisms which often precipitate asthmatic attacks. This was clearly validated in an American study of japa yoga in 22 asthmatic patients.[2] At the end of three months of daily practice of japa, 94% of the patients had improved airway resistance compared to a control group. They continued to take their routine medications, but reported that the severity of their symptoms was reduced. The patients' own doctors were asked to assess their clinical condition. 55% felt that their patient's condition had improved after meditation, while 27% thought their patient's condition was worse. However, 74% of the patients themselves reported that meditation had benefited their asthma, 69% felt it had improved their general health and 68% felt it had improved their emotional life.

3. Yoga nidra and asthma

Relaxation has been used by a Texas paediatrician to cure six adolescents who were severe asthma sufferers.[3] These children learned to induce the yoga nidra state of deep relaxation by conjuring up a pleasing mental image. One boy pictured himself running along and breathing freely as his lungs cleared out. After learning yoga nidra, all six children still suffered from asthma attacks, but these were shorter, less frequent and required fewer visits to the doctor or hospital. All six children stopped taking medication without adverse effects. All the children remained improved at seven months follow-up and were continuing to practise yoga nidra whenever they felt the need to do so. The boy who visualized himself running even won a race in real life.

In all investigations, the results are better for sufferers who adopt yoga soon after the onset of the disease, before it has developed into a severe, chronic stage. Those with asthma are recommended to commence yoga training as soon as possible after the initial attack.

Bronchitis and emphysema

There are two other conditions in which the bronchial tubes are obstructed and respiration is impaired. Chronic bronchitis refers to long-term inflammation of the bronchial tubes, with phlegm production and a moist, productive cough. Emphysema is a degenerative condition of the lungs themselves, which become permanently hyperinflated due to excessive dilation of the air sacs (alveoli).

These twin conditions usually occur in middle and later life in men who are chronic smokers. Their condition generally continues to deteriorate steadily in spite of medical management. Patients commonly degenerate into 'respiratory cripples' with constant air hunger even at rest, and require continual physiotherapy and postural drainage of pooled mucous secretions from the lungs.

Chronic obstructive airways disease (COAD) study

In 1978, Dr M.K. Tandon, a physician from Western Australia, published an account of an experimental trial with 22 elderly patients suffering with severe symptoms of these conditions, termed chronic obstructive airways disease (COAD). His report appeared in the journal *Thorax*.[4] Half of these patients received routine physiotherapy treatment, while the other half received yoga training. Tandon found that at the end of nine months, the yoga trained subjects exhibited:
- Improved exercise tolerance
- Quicker recovery after exertion
- Ability to control an attack of shortness of breath without requiring medical assistance
- Definite improvement in overall chest condition

The breathing pattern of the yoga trained group was changed to a more efficient one. It was deeper and slower in comparison with their original condition before the experiment with yoga, and in comparison with the continued shallow, fast breathing of the physiotherapy group, which showed no improvement in the breathing pattern.

90

We must remember too that these are severe diseases in elderly people, who under usual conditions would have further deteriorated during the nine months of the investigations, rather than improving as well as they did with yoga. The role of yoga in the future medical management of COAD is assured because it offers a unique opportunity for improvement even in severe lung incapacity.

Effects of asana and pranayama

The value of yoga asanas in improving the various components of respiratory efficiency such as vital capacity (VC), forced expiratory volume in 1 second (FEV 1) and total lung capacity (TLC) was demonstrated in a Soviet study of professional gymnasts who performed 5 major yogasanas – sirshasana, mayurasana, chakrasana, sarvangasana and halasana.[5] In distinction from ordinary exercise programs, asanas were found to demand a much lower energy consumption, and demand only slight increase in oxygen consumption, while concurrently leading to markedly improved lung capacity and volumes – a crucial point.

For example, the increased oxygen consumption required in merely changing from a sitting position to walking slowly at 2 m.p.h. is 230%. This is a large increase ($2^{1}/_{3}$ times), suggesting that the increase demanded in performing normal 'energetic exercises' would be enormous in comparison, far beyond the capacities of those with respiratory impairment. However, the Russians discovered that the oxygen consumption in sirshasana rose from 288 ml./min. to 665 ml./min., i.e. about 130%, while another study of sirshasana conducted in India with experienced yogic subjects detected an increase of oxygen consumption during sirshasana of only 48%.[6] This means that sirshasana consumes only $1/4$ to $1/2$ of the oxygen demanded by slow walking, while it simultaneously improves respiratory capacity and lung function.

Clearly yoga asanas play a vital role in the rehabilitation and the management of bronchitis and emphysematous patients, especially where respiratory reserve is reduced even to the extent of being unable to walk slowly. What other practice except yoga can restore such a depleted lung capacity?

Pranayama is actually the most important discipline in recovery and rehabilitation of sufferers from chronic respiratory impairment. It is possible to overhaul and restore even those states of highly disrupted respiratory behaviour and imbalance which occur in chronic respiratory failure. Many months may be required, but yoga definitely has the capacity to restore an ailing respiratory system and progressively reverse and restore a grossly disturbed cardio-respiratory ratio.

The normal respiratory rate is about 15 breaths per minute (see discussion on respiratory ratios). The respiratory cripple may be forced to breathe 30 or more times per minute, and still be short of breath. In order to systematically reverse and harness the breath and restore respiratory functional capacity, various distinct types of pranayama are useful. These include bhramari, ujjayi, kapalbhati and bhastrika pranayamas. When the various pranayamas are performed correctly, they have been found to demand only a marginal increase in oxygen consumption over normal quiet breathing.[7] This increase has been measured to be between 12% and 35%. Compare this to slow walking which demands a 230% increase, and it becomes clear that pranayama is an essential step in recovery from COAD, where diminished respiratory reserve precludes even walking.

Pranayamas such as kapalbhati and bhastrika are not difficult to perform, either for a novice or a sufferer from COAD. However, they should be practised differently by each, according to his differing respiratory capacity.

Chronic obstructive airways disease (COAD)
In chronic obstructive airways disease the patient's capacity to exert himself is minimal. He is poised on the brink of respiratory failure, often depending for his life upon daily

drainage of the lungs by physiotherapy, and frequent enrichment of his oxygen supply by provision of a readily accessible oxygen mask. He is a true cripple, suffering constant air hunger, even at rest. Even walking is a major effort, and normal exercise, which demands some degree of respiratory reserve capacity to commence with, is impossible.

Yogic training for these patients offers the only real possibility of improvement, as indicated by Dr Tandon's remarkable trial, which extended over a nine month period.

From our own experience, sufferers from chronic bronchitis and emphysema who take up yoga respond remarkably well to it. I am not only talking about the elderly respiratory cripples, but more importantly about the young and middle-aged heavy smokers who appear destined for the same fate later on in life.

Yoga program for chronic obstructive airways disease (COAD)

1. *Asana*: Pawanmuktasana part 1, performed slowly according to capacity, allowing time for rest. Vajrasana and shashankasana, gradually introducing the head down position and slowly increasing its duration. Advasana is the best posture for relaxation and yoga nidra. It allows the drainage of the lungs, and should be practised with the foot of the bed elevated, if this can be tolerated.
   In mild to moderate states, the following asanas should also be adopted: hasta utthanasana, surya namaskara, pawanmuktasana part 3, shashank bhujangasana, vipareeta karani mudra, sarvangasana, halasana, paschimottanasana, ushtrasana.
2. *Pranayama*: Ujjayi, bhramari, bhastrika and kapalbhati.
3. *Shatkarma*: Kunjal and neti kriyas daily.
4. *Meditation*: Ajapa japa/antar mouna.
5. *Relaxation*: Yoga nidra in shavasana or any comfortable position.

Question 12

Cancer

In Chamarande in 1980, I heard your discussion on the application of yoga in cancer. Please speak more about this. In what fields has it been tried? Which techniques are used? What medical controls have these patients submitted to?

When I was a child, cancer was virtually unknown. It was a rare occurrence. Perhaps 5 people in 100 died from it. At that time tuberculosis was a mystery to medical scientists, and it was a greatly feared condition, much as cancer is today. Of course, medical science has advanced since then, and now tuberculosis is a curable disorder.

Today the spectrum of disease has evolved and a new situation confronts us. Cancer is now the 'death sentence disease'; 1/3 of deaths are attributed to it, and this is rising rapidly. Cancer now evokes fear in the mind of modern man, while its cause remains a mystery to researchers.

Both yogic and medical sciences recognize cancer as a state of cellular anarchy, but our points of view differ a little as to the cause. Medical science has focused its attention upon the cancer cells themselves and also upon their environment. They have succeeded in isolating some of the contributing causes. These have been called carcinogens: chemical dyes, food preservatives, cigarette smoke, atmospheric pollution and low fibre diet are just a few of them.

On the other hand, yoga has come to the conclusion that cancer originates on the mental plane as a deeply ingrained process of anarchical or self-destructive thinking. Whereas most of the psychosomatic diseases follow a recognizable code of behaviour, cancer is a total exception to the role. Most diseases give rise to pain and other symptoms early, but cancer grows insidiously for many years, unrecognized and undetected.

Most diseases manifest as part of the body's inbuilt mechanism of self-preservation. They are usually self-limiting and lead to greater cellular resistance as a direct result. They represent the body's response to a 'healthy mind' which remains neurotically loyal to nature's laws, and initiates self-correcting diseases as a direct result.

Cancer belongs to a different dimension of disease altogether. It comes not to restore balance in the body, but to kill the body, at a stage when the anarchical mind's self-destructive tendencies have proved incorrigible, and natural law has been flouted for many years.

Can cancer be cured?

This is the overwhelming question confronting medical science. Thousands of researchers and billions of dollars are devoted exclusively to pursuing the answer. What we need to know is whether yoga has something to offer.

'Spontaneous remission', the inexplicable regression of cancer for months or years, has been seen in a small number of cases. Similarly, there have always been myriad 'cancer cures', which have undoubtedly proved successful in isolated cases, even though the precise scientific mechanism of these cures is unclear to us. These therapies are diverse indeed. They include grape juice, sunlight therapy, holy water, apricot seeds, prayers and wheat grass. These are just a few among thousands which have been unable to stand up to scientific scrutiny. They are unscientific and therefore unacceptable to many of us. They may appear quaint, amusing and preposterous, but let us not doubt that they have been instrumental in cancer cures in the past, even if the precise mechanism involved still remains elusive. At the same time, let us also remember that the medical profession has scarcely fared better in cancer management, using the most advanced techniques of surgery, irradiation and chemotherapy.

The role of yoga in cancer therapy

I am well aware of the situation in cancer research, and I have been conducting my own trials by using yoga with different forms of cancer for many years. Many patients have been helped even when all hope of recovery had been abandoned. Yoga has invariably proved effective, and even where death has been inevitable, yoga has nevertheless bestowed relief, palliation, hope and courage, and an extension of life as well.

Five year incubation period

As you know, the crucial period in cancer is five years. It takes five years and usually longer for cancer to be recognized and diagnosed after its conception. Perhaps it originates in a single thought and a single cell. The proliferation of this tiny focus of insurrection against the natural balance and order continues at an exponential rate for five years before detection. During this period, these latently evolving cancers can be eradicated. There is every reason to believe that a basically loyal mind frequently spawns destructive ideas, and cancer foci result, but these are overcome by the body's self-surveillance systems as a matter of course.

The preventative role of yoga must be considered here, especially the hatha yoga shatkriyas, such as shankhaprakshalana, which periodically purify the whole gastrointestinal tract, both as curative, preventative and cautionary measures. The individual who adopts a yogic lifestyle of asana, pranayama and meditation has the best possible guarantee of a cancer-free future. There is little doubt about this.

96

Five year survival rate

Secondly, the effectiveness of cancer treatments is assessed by the five year survival rate. This refers to the number of patients still living free from cancer recurrence five years after initial diagnosis and treatment. The results for all forms of cancer therapy in most types of cancer remain fairly poor to date, although there have been a few promising developments.

The incorporation of yoga practices, including yoga nidra and meditation, into the existing treatment regimes for cancer offers the best prospect for improving the five year survival rates for the existing forms of therapy, including fasting, dietary modification, surgery and irradiation. This will be borne out in clinical trials in the future. A number of pioneering studies have already been conducted and their results are promising. They show that yoga definitely has a powerful inhibiting influence upon cancer, and will effectively augment the conventional therapeutic regimes.

The next step is to conduct larger trials in which two groups of patients participate. The first group should receive conventional management, but no yoga. In this way the scientific evidence will emerge and many lives may be saved in the future.

INTENSIVE MEDITATION

Meditation offers the best prospect for inducing a remission after cancer has been diagnosed. The best results are obtained when intensive meditation is combined with pranayama, asanas, and dietary regulation. Meditation induces a change in the depressed outlook of the cancer patient. Severe depression and anxiety almost always complicate the patient's condition and worsen the outlook. Meditation invariably produces a change in outlook. Depression lowers the immune defences and the diminished white cell count reflects this. Meditation and yoga practices bolster the immune responses, increase the resistance and transform the patient's outlook. This is the first step on the path to remission.

Quantity and quality of life

Cancer patients suffer most by being unable to accept the prospect of their own death. They cling to their remaining life obsessively, without realizing that the quality of remaining life is more important than its quantity. Much of the pain and suffering in cancer arises on the psychological plane, where the individual mind, by aching for its own permanence, actually accelerates its demise.

The success of meditation in cancer therapy should not be assessed only in terms of the extension of lifetime it bestows, but also upon the capacity to improve the quality of experience of the terminal weeks and months of life.

Meditation brings peace, acceptance and detachment

Meditation is the practice of increasing the awareness so that a greater vision of the truth will be known to us. It is a process in which our false perceptions and illusions, including those about life and death, are realized. In treating cancer, intensive meditation of several hours per day may be necessary to evolve these terminal patients rapidly to a level of awareness where they can accept their situation. The real fruit of meditation for the cancer patient is the realization that it is his attachment to life at any price which is his real disease.

Maladaptive response to life

Cancer begins with a maladaptive response, either psychological or physiological, earlier in life, which has become established and entrenched in the lifestyle and pattern of thinking. During meditation, patients experience a deeper, prelogical level of awareness. They undergo a form of regression of mental functioning, going back into earlier life and experience, and ablating past maladaptive responses.

This is accompanied by a similar regression of physiological function in which the usual homeostatic control mechanisms are re-established.

Meditation posture is important

Patients should sit motionless in a meditation posture for one or more hours every day. This may appear to be a cruel procedure to impose upon a weakened and suffering person. However, it is actually a crucial and important aspect of the therapy, for the determination of the patient is aroused and this is most important in future prognosis. As meditation therapy progresses, physical discomfort is transcended.

Meditation enhances awareness

During the process of meditation therapy, a profound reaction occurs in cancer patients. Those who have succeeded in resisting and overcoming cancer have invariably come to a different, more meaningful experience of life. This change is not just a philosophical or ethical one, but is a direct reflection of a higher state of awareness. It is first noticed as a subtle change in the patient's behaviour. His relatives and friends comment that he has in some way changed himself, become a better person with greater awareness and understanding. They report, "He no longer gets so upset; he is not worried about the cancer like before."

These outer manifestations are the direct effects of inner changes in the individual's level of spiritual integration. They are mirrored in altered physiological parameters and an improved clinical situation which often allows the patient to add many more fruitful months and years to his life. This extension or parole period, in which remission of cancer occurs either permanently or temporarily, is a direct result of meditation. During these extra days the patient definitely evolves a greater understanding of his environment and his illness. This is the crucial turning-point in any struggle with cancer. The awareness undergoes a fundamental change. He no longer sinks into self-pity and frustration but becomes aware of the active role he plays in getting sick and being well.

The next crucial step in meditation occurs when the patient becomes more interested in his changed experience of life than in his cancer. The relief of his cancer becomes a side effect of a greater experience. Now he is no longer obsessed with it. It becomes just a bonus that may eventuate. This new state of mind is responsible for remarkable regression of advanced cancers, and even their complete disappearance in some patients.

Yoga nidra in cancer therapy

Yoga nidra can be adopted as a form of therapy in cancer of all stages. It is especially useful in conjunction with meditation therapy. Yoga nidra sessions in shavasana should follow the sessions of intensive meditation in the sitting posture. In this way a balance between concentration and relaxation is established.

Yoga nidra is a very rapid way of realizing the mind's capacities to heal, to create, to visualize, to destroy. Meditation induces a state of concentrated effort in which witness awareness is preserved so that knowledge of the nature of reality dawns directly in the consciousness. Yoga nidra, on the other hand, is a process of creative surrender, a giving up of all preconceptions in order to let the awareness drift of its own volition like a piece of driftwood upon the ocean. Meditation involves effort, while yoga nidra involves relaxation, surrender and letting go.

Yoga nidra has been specifically adapted for cancer therapy in a number of ways. In the first place, the former life, memories and experiences can be exploded from the subconscious mind so that defective past maladaptions can be recognized and corrected. This can be facilitated by using imagery and symbols to awaken the deeper subconscious and suppressed memories and fantasies.

Secondly, the awakening and mobilization of pranic (bioplasmic) energy and its conscious direction throughout the body is developed. In tantra, this science is termed prana vidya. It is one whole system of sadhana which opens up in the deeper stages of yoga nidra. This is the basis of psychic, pranic, mental and spiritual healing. Thirdly, a link between yoga nidra and prana vidya is developed by conscious visualization of healing forces and forms of various types. Healing may be visualized as a flow of light or energy directed within the physical body. This begins as an imagination and becomes an experience as practice proceeds. This is called pranic healing.

Healing can also be precipitated purely on the mental plane by creative fantasy and image visualization. Here the cancer is visualized shrinking in size; the army of white blood cells is conjured up and sent into battle with the cancer cells; the body is seen again and again in perfect health, and so on. This is mental healing.

Power of sankalpa

The final application of yoga nidra is in development of willpower. In healing cancer, an enormous endurance capacity and willpower is necessary. This is gained by using a sankalpa during yoga nidra.

Sankalpa means 'personal resolution', that which I seek to realize most in my life. It is formulated as a short positive statement and is repeated mentally again and again with full identification, full conviction, full faith that this is the reality I am forging in my life. It is released like a seed into the subconscious mind at specific times during the practice, while the experience of relaxation is very deep and the subconscious mind is laid bare and accessible.

Sankalpa is a most powerful way of transforming the lifestyle and bringing about specific results. It has always been known and used in tantra for various purposes. It works because it mobilizes a mighty force – the subconscious will, and brings it into conscious awareness. Some may say it is a form of hypnosis or brain-washing, and perhaps it may be. But do not forget that it is your own self which has

101

formulated your own sankalpa – it is what you really want. Therefore, it is your own self who is washing your brain and it is your own self who is doing the hypnotizing.

Our own research studies over many years have shown us beyond doubt that yoga nidra can bring about even the impossible in life. Cancer patients should practise it under skilled guidance, in conjunction with pranayama, meditation, dietary control, fasting and amaroli.

Research studies

The work of Dr Ainslie Meares, an Australian psychiatrist, is most impressive and bears out our own research. He demonstrated clear regression of cancer of the rectum following intensive meditation[1] and also the remission of massive metastases (secondary cancers) from a primary undifferentiated carcinoma of the lung, associated with meditation therapy.[2] Another of his case histories reported in the *Medical Journal of Australia* clearly illustrated the regression of cancer after intensive meditation.[3] The form of meditation used by Meares is a combination of japa, nada yoga and yoga nidra.

Significant clinical trials of meditation and visualization have also been reported by other researchers. Dr O.C. Simonton, a radiotherapist from Texas, found that meditation significantly increased the lifespan of cancer patients undergoing radiotherapy in a controlled trial.[4] He has found that patients can bolster their immune response by visualizing their white blood cells actively attacking and destroying the cancer cells.[5]

AMAROLI

There is another practice which we sometimes recommend for cancer and other serious disorders. This is known in tantra as amaroli or shivambu kalpa – auto-urine therapy. It can be combined with fasting under skilled guidance. For best results, all the urine should then be utilized.

Amaroli cannot be practised where:
- The diet contains animal products or processed and refined foods.
- The patient is receiving drugs or other medications. However, it can be discontinued and resumed again after courses of conventional therapies, if desired.

The role of poisons

According to medical science, urine is toxic and poisonous, but in yogic science we recognize that poisons are sometimes necessary and useful if they are correctly administered. In order to disarm a poison, it is sometimes necessary to use a poison. It is the same as many modern drugs, which will often produce side effects of diarrhoea, vomiting, skin rash, deafness, liver disturbance, etc. Are these not poisons? Yet we recognize that in certain situations they should be prescribed. For a healthy individual, digitalis is a poison, but for a coronary patient it is a life-saving drug. In the same way, urine should be taken by the cancer patient.

Remember that the mind and body of a cancer patient do not reflect the normal balance. Whereas a fundamentally healthy person possesses some forms of mental neurosis and anxiety and, as a result, develops symptoms of normal psychosomatic diseases at different stages in life, cancer is a different process altogether. Here there is a state of mental and cellular psychosis going on, in which there has been a complete takeover of the body's existing order and also a subversion of its inbuilt immune defence mechanisms.

In order to rid the body and mind of this anarchical state of affairs, it is necessary to initiate not just a psychological transformation, but a complete psycho-physiological upheaval. This can best be precipitated by the practice of amaroli.

Urine can be taken internally and applied externally. We have recommended it even in severe fungating cancers, with remarkable results, but as yet the precise immuno-logical mechanisms of amaroli remain to be defined. Amaroli definitely has a role to play in cancer therapy in future years and the time has come for medical science to give it serious consideration. After all, prostaglandins are derived from animal urine, penicillin is extracted from a mould – no one questions that these are valuable and vital substances. Then how is it that we can see no value in our own body's secretions?

Urine is an ultrafiltrate of the blood

The urine is not in the same classification as the body's solid wastes. Rather it is an ultrafiltrate of the blood – sterile and antiseptic. Of course, in a high protein diet consisting of meat, eggs, milk, etc., the urine has a high concentration of urea and ammonia – the protein wastes. Such urine is offensive. But this is not the diet we recommend with amaroli. In fact, animal products, including milk, butter, etc. are absolutely contraindicated in all forms of cancer, but especially where amaroli is to be practised.

Tantric medicine

Amaroli is an important practice in the tantric tradition. The tantric text *Damara Tantra* is devoted to the use of urine for healing purposes and gives the methods of preparing and using urine in order to overcome diseases and their tendencies in the body and mind. The text describes urine as shivambu – the divine nectar of Lord Shiva. The person who completes the practice of amaroli is said in that text to attain the state of divine consciousness of Lord Shiva himself.

From the point of view of medical science, amaroli is a means of initiating a major healing crisis within a depleted body, so that the individual's own capacities to overcome the cancer are mobilized. Amaroli is traditionally practised in secret, in isolation, together with prolonged fasting and meditation, which potentiate its effects. It is practised by those who have a deep-seated or insidious disease which remains incurable by more conventional means.

In India, people who fall sick with such terminal diseases as cancer do not admit themselves to hospital in order to have all their cares attended to while they die. Rather, they retire from active life and go to an isolated place where they can practise amaroli, fasting and meditation until they are cured.

Even those who perish in the struggle to rid the body of cancer are provided with the best possible opportunity to realize the defective subconscious conditioning which has led them to reject or abuse a part of their natural capacities. As they recognize and accept this, a new vision of reality descends and they die in a state of natural intoxication, free from pain, with dignity and awareness, in the lap of Lord Shiva.

How amaroli works

The precise mechanism of action in amaroli remains to be clearly defined by future researchers. However, the practice appears to initiate a process of psychophysiological renewal in the following way:

Psychological overhaul: recognition and overhaul of the wayward thinking patterns of the mind can be precipitated by first bringing the subconscious mind clearly into consciousness. Then the errors in thinking, belief, etc. which have precipitated cancer's development, can be seen, recognized and corrected in meditation.

Most often, cancer arises out of a failure to recognize and accept some aspect of life, and this is reflected in rejection of, or failure to accept, the functions of the interrelated bodily organs. For example, cancer of the rectum, breast or uterus may originate in a feeling that these organs are associated with dirty or unnatural functions.

In yoga we recognize that the human body belongs to nature's kingdom, and that it is in no way inherently dirty. The source of dirt is in the perverted, suppressed and wrongly conditioned mind. Amaroli, especially when practised with fasting and meditation, is the quickest way to dissolve the barrier or veil between the conscious and subconscious mind.

How we perceive the urine really depends on the purity of our own consciousness. If we perceive it as dirty, it is either because our lifestyle, habits and diet are impure, or else we are victims of mental preconditioning. Once we are clean in our physical and mental habits, the urine indeed becomes a nectar, capable of rapidly eliminating even cancer from the body.

Physiological upheaval: The second aspect of amaroli is its physiological impact upon the body. The contents of the urine reflect our diet and also our metabolism. Its constituents depend on our mental and emotional states in the hours before we pass that urine. The urine is known to contain many vital hormone molecules and their breakdown products, including the prostaglandins, the adrenal 'stress' hormones and the steroids and sex hormones. In this sense, the urine collected from the bladder is a sensitive and accurate indicator of our psychological and physiological behaviour and reactions during that time period.

The period of dream sleep each night is one in which the subconscious mind is laid open. Although we remain consciously unaware of this, the activity of our dreams is nevertheless mirrored in the hormonal contents of the first urine passed in the morning. This urine is especially recommended for cancer patients. By reassimilating this urine, recognition of subconscious blockages and defective conditioning can be precipitated.

Negative feedback pathway

The growth of various cancers, especially of the breast and reproductive organs, is known to be influenced by excessive levels of sexual hormones in the blood. Many other hormones are also known to actively inhibit or stimulate cancer growth. It may well be that by reassimilating the breakdown products of these hormones, a 'negative feedback' effect is created, which limits further secretion of

106

those hormones from the endocrine glands and creates an unfavourable milieu for further cancer growth.

Both fasting[6] and meditation[7] have been shown to increase the levels of steroid breakdown products in the urine, and to increase the body's stress resistance, and amaroli probably potentiates the actions of these practices.

Amaroli poisons cancer cells

Cancer cells are known to replicate profusely and uncontrollably because they operate with an unfair physiological advantage over the normal body cells. Cancer cells defy the existing order of constraints upon normal cells – that the overall good of the organism as a whole is the most important factor in determining cellular behaviour. Cancer starts when a single wayward cell begins to live for itself alone. This cell rapidly divides, and its daughter cells grow and divide preferentially also, soon coming to consume a high proportion of nutrients intended for the whole tissue or organ. So it is that a terminal cancer patient is emaciated, undernourished and weak, while the cancer alone continues to thrive, consuming the nutrients of the whole organism.

Simultaneously, the metabolic wastes of the cancer cells are far in excess of those of the other, starving body cells. In amaroli we employ the principle of smothering the cancer cells in their own wastes, to which they are more sensitive than the other body cells. As a result the cancer cells die of exposure to their own poisons more quickly than the normal body cells, which have adapted themselves for survival and become resistant to the high levels of cancerous wastes in their environment.

This principle is identical to the rationale used by modern oncologists who use the most potent poisons such as nitrogen mustard, or irradiate the body with high levels of radioactivity, knowing that the cancer cells are less resistant to these poisons and will be more greatly damaged than the normal body cells. However, amaroli is more effective in this regard as it is a natural body product.

When amaroli is practised in greater and greater concentrations, while other nourishment is minimized or discontinued, the cancer cells are the most severely afflicted, for they have no prior exposure or resistance to their own stench and smell. The rest of the body cells survive this trial because the mind at last glimpses the opportunity to be rid of the long-time oppressor. They resist and struggle on like underground resistance fighters in an overrun and occupied country, as there is great strength to be had in resisting together a force of great might.

These cells have the benefit of prior exposure to the cancer's poisons, as they have had to endure them and live in them in increasing concentration for at least five years beforehand. They have acquired resistance because they have suffered so long in silence, like the conquered people under an occupying army. They have learned to survive on very little, while the oppressor has always taken the wealth of the land for itself.

Once amaroli is commenced with complete conviction, the oppressors must give up. Once their food supply dries up, there is only an increasing supply of their own poison, to which they are highly sensitive. They must inevitably die.

Amaroli is drastic therapy for a drastic disease. It does not guarantee cure of the cancer and preservation of the physical body. That depends on the strength of the patient's resistance, faith and endurance, in comparison to the degree of entrenchment of the tumour. Nevertheless it does offer one of the best prospects for cure. Medical science should not delay in investigating this practice further.

Yogic Methods in Cardiopulmonary Diseases*

Yoga is an ancient science of both mental and physical health, as well as aiming to fulfil the potential of man. Physical and mental health are side effects of the total yogic process. From the medical point of view we can define yoga as a scientific system by which we can manipulate our internal environment, both physical and mental. We believe that yoga can help us to gain control of our nervous system and can stimulate the internal production and secretion of chemicals and also turn off these secretions at will.

Apart from its incorporation into ayurveda, the application of yoga purely to disease situations is one of its newest facets. However, it appears that yoga can offer us much in this area, considering the epidemic proportions of degenerative and psychosomatic diseases such as coronary artery disease, hypertension, diabetes, asthma, cancer and so on. The Bihar School of Yoga has been assessing yoga's role in these diseases and formulating appropriate regimes of therapy based on the basic principles of yoga.

---

*This is a modified version of a guest lecture delivered by Dr Swami Shankardevananda Saraswati MBBS (Sydney) at the International Congress on Cardiovascular Diseases, Calcutta, 12th–15th January, 1984. Organized by East Indian Chapter, International Academy of Chest Physicians and Surgeons, American College of Chest Physicians.

At present, as medical sciences have no cure for these diseases and can offer only palliative relief, it is our duty as doctors and 'healers' to look into any claim that may offer relief from our present predicament. It is yoga's claim that we have a choice: either degeneration via our present mode of living and medicine, or regeneration via yoga.

Misconceptions

It is important to realize what yoga is not, for many misconceptions have grown up around this science, many of which are founded upon ignorance and supposition rather than trial and experience.

Yoga is not a religion, nor is it renunciation. Yoga is a system of balancing body, mind and consciousness and is meant for those living amidst the strain and tension of everyday living. It is a method of harmonizing the inner and outer aspect of our being.

Yoga does not demand that we have to get up at 4 am, be a vegetarian, give up smoking, drinking alcohol and so on. Of course, these suggestions are made to those who are interested in going more deeply into the yogic sciences, in preventing disease, maintaining good health and peace of mind, and developing higher awareness. However, they are not prerequisites for yoga, and indeed, once the basic principles of yoga are learned, practised and understood, we can use every situation in life to develop ourselves and to grow into better human beings. Yoga can be applied anywhere, anytime, at work, at home or even in such meetings as we are having right here and now. This should, for better results, be combined with a small program of daily practice.

Another misconception is that yoga is physical exercise. This is also incorrect. Yoga possesses many techniques which have effects at the physical, emotional, mental, psychic and spiritual levels of our being. Yoga transcends mere physical exercise by incorporating relaxation, breathing and energizing components, as well as the development of

110

awareness. It develops our awareness of who we are physically, mentally and spiritually; and good health, strength, vitality, concentration, peace of mind, satisfaction, self-control etc. are all side effects of the total yogic process.

Quality of life

One of the great dilemmas faced by physicians is how to treat the disease and at the same time improve the quality of the patient's life. Often we save a life but the quality of life that person faces is perhaps worse than death. We really have no choice in this matter within our present system of medicine. What is required is an expanded concept of total patient care.

Total patient care means that we treat the patient at the physical, emotional and mental levels. We know, for example, that tension and stress are huge factors in precipitating not only cardiovascular diseases, but almost all forms of psychosomatic and degenerative disease. Though we are all aware of the role of stress, tension, mental dissatisfaction, the type 'A' personality, and so on, in the aetiology of heart disease, so far there is no effective means to combat this aspect; nothing has been applied in practice to help patients reduce stress and tension. This is where yoga comes into the foreground.

The mind is, as yet, an unknown factor in our lives. We do not know exactly what it is but we are beginning to appreciate its powerful and far-reaching effects. One of yoga's major contributions to medicine will probably be its exact and practical definitions of mind – its relationship to the body – and the techniques to relax, tame, control and utilize this vast and potent force.

Together with our medicines, surgery and other body-based approaches to health, we require yoga, meditation, relaxation, simple exercise, dietary and lifestyle advice and correction, and perhaps even acupuncture, herbs and massage, to try to reconstruct a totally healthy and better human being. We have a vast armamentarium to choose from if we want to give them a fair trial, many of which will definitely beneficially improve health and well-being, to some extent at least.

Yoga offers us methods which can relax, energize and strengthen body and psyche if they are properly taught and practised. These techniques can be combined with medicines and in no way conflict with traditional forms of therapy. Rather, they complement them and may even prove to be more than additive in their effect.

Yoga and medicine

It is important to remember that, unlike many other natural methods of healing, yoga accepts all systems of therapy which are valid and useful. It can and should work in conjunction with, and not as a replacement for drugs, surgery or any other necessary form of treatment.

Modern medicine is a great science, so is yoga. If we take the best of both systems we can amalgamate a new and better system that offers more relief from disease and more satisfaction to both the patient and the doctor. For example, we require drugs to help reduce high blood pressure in the short-term. However, no one looks forward to a lifetime of drug therapy, the possible side effects of medication and the almost inevitable sequelae of the disease process.

The present inability of medicine to prevent and cure the majority of psychosomatic diseases is a great stressor for both doctor and patient. The prospect of a lifetime of drug therapy and ongoing progressive disease and disability is a source of great anxiety to the patient and is a major factor in speeding up the degenerative process. Our impotence in this situation is a potent stressor and source of anxiety for the doctor also. It is yoga's claim and challenge that we do not always have to accept this situation and that we can arrest, ameliorate and perhaps even cure the disease process by systematic and scientific application of a few simple physical postures (asana), breathing techniques (pranayama) and relaxation-type meditative techniques.

112

The yoga centre or ashram stands as a referral centre where patients, having been previously investigated, diagnosed and treated by a medical professional, can learn to relax and improve their awareness and perception by yoga and receive support through the initial and critical stage of their therapy – the yoga teacher usually having more time to give to the student than the doctor. Progress must be followed up medically and alterations made by the physician over appropriate periods of time until they are considered disease-free.

One very important point is that yoga and medicine in combination will have a much better chance of working if the disease is managed in its early stage, before complications arise, and usually in younger patients. Doctors should remember this and recommend yoga for chronic psychosomatic and stress-induced diseases as soon as they are diagnosed and before they have a chance to progress; prevention being better and easier than cure. Though doctors themselves may not wish to practise or teach yoga, it is vital that they give their patients a chance and inform them of the possible benefits and advantages of incorporating a few simple yogic practices into their lives. People should know of the alternatives; they should have a choice.

Dr Jonas Salk has said, "Medicine is the science of disease. Yoga is the science of health. How then can medicine examine the claims of yoga?" The claims of yoga can be examined if we allow yoga to prove itself in well thought out and planned experimental trials, many of which have already been done.[1-7] We are also doing these at the Bihar School of Yoga and are planning a joint research project to assess the role of relaxation tapes in Intensive Care and Intermediate Coronary Care Units.

Psychophysiology of yoga
Yoga exerts its effects on both the body and mind. It affects the tissues locally and centrally. For example, asanas work by flexing and extending the tissues locally so as to

stimulate nerves, blood, lymph, endocrine organs, glands and neural plexuses. Local compression of various structures affects the whole body. Pranayama and meditation, on the other hand, appear to work centrally and the effects spread to the periphery.

It is well-known that yoga is a powerful method to induce relaxation and is, therefore, one of the best antidotes to stress. It is more than likely that it does this via its neuroendocrine effects.[8-12] There are many studies which point to yoga's capacity to influence the brain, to increase alpha wave activity in the frontal lobes, indicating relaxation of the thinking processes, to increase theta wave activity, which seems to indicate enhanced creativity, imagery and insight, and generally to synchronize, harmonize and integrate brain functioning.

There is also good research on yoga's ability to influence pain, and this is very important from the cardiovascular point of view.[13-14] This research seems to indicate that yoga can dissociate prefrontal lobe activity from the limbic system and thereby alter our emotional response to pain and stressful situations in general. When emotional energy can be dissociated from negative thinking it can be transmuted from fear, anxiety, and so on, and, according to yoga, utilized for positive, creative and healing activity and the expansion of awareness. This is an essential step in yoga's systematic approach to palliation and eventual cure of cardiovascular disease.

In terms of cardiovascular disease, yogic practices acting centrally would relax the autonomic nervous system and, we can hypothesize, improve blockage of the sympathetic system. They may, therefore, augment the effects of beta-blockers and this would then be a good argument for the use of certain techniques even in the acute myocardial infarct situation, in the intensive care ward.

There is good evidence that stress affects the immune system and studies seem to point out the fact that relaxation and, therefore, yoga should also exert its influence at this level.[15] We can assume that any system which beneficially affects the three major controlling systems of the body will contribute to overall psychophysiological health and would then be a powerful factor in many types of cardiorespiratory problems, thus contributing to total patient health.

Yogic techniques for the heart

There are two main yogic approaches to cardiovascular disease by yoga. The first is the classical situation where one learns a series of techniques and performs them twice or more times daily. Over a period of time, the benefits can be felt to extend throughout the day, helping us to relax, face and handle stress, deal more effectively with people and situations in general, and feel better within ourselves.

The second is a modified approach for busy people such as executives and doctors, who are particularly prone to cardiovascular disease and probably need yoga and relaxation more than people who have the time to do it. The basic principles of yoga are taught and then applied at work and at home during activity and for a few minutes in the morning and evening before sleep. This does not require much time and delivers a wonderful improvement in the quality of life, ameliorating the disease process. The morning and evening practice program can be extended as desired by the patient.

The following regime has been used at Bihar School of Yoga in the majority of cases of heart disease with success:

1. *Pawanmuktasana part 1* (modified): These are simple, gentle stretching exercises, all performed slowly, without any strain, and synchronized with slow, gentle, relaxed breathing and awareness. By combining movement with breathing and awareness, we engage, align and rebalance both the body and the mind, and this is the key to success through yogic techniques. This series of asanas can be used in hospital; however, it is contraindicated in the acute myocardial infarct situation. It is a cardiovascular rehabilitative series which may help to develop collateral

115

circulation without putting a strain on the heart. It is progressive and graduated and probably the best series for the majority of therapeutic situations. Other major asanas should not be used in cardiovascular disease unless under expert guidance.

2. *Nadi shodhana pranayama*: This is slow, rhythmic, alternate nostril breathing in the ratio of one to one, or one to two, inhalation to exhalation. This superimposes a soothing, rhythmic breath onto the cardiorespiratory system which quickly slows the heart rate and beneficially affects rhythmicity of the heart.

Shannahoff-Khalsa of the Davis Center for Behavioral Neurobiology, Salk Institute for Biological Studies, San Diego, USA and his co-workers, have demonstrated the first conclusive evidence linking alternating hemispheric dominance, the autonomic nervous systems and the breathing cycle.[16] The breath in the nostrils fluctuates every 1–3 hours on average. Shannahoff-Khalsa has shown that when the right nostril is dominant, the left hemisphere is also, and vice versa.[17]

His studies, when substantiated, may lend credence to the claims of yogis that breathing through the left nostril stimulates the right hemisphere and vice versa and that the individual has the 'ability to non-invasively, selectively and predictably alter cerebral activity and associated physiological processes'.[18] The implications for our overall health from this study are staggering and seem to indicate that a few simple breathing techniques may be able to alter our neurophysiology, metabolic functions and state of mind. This practice is also contraindicated in the first few days of acute myocardial infarction.

3. *Bhramari pranayama*: This technique involves making a humming sound while blocking the ears. It is a powerful yogic tranquillizer, and quickly allays anxiety. We believe it acts on the limbic-hypothalamic-pituitary-autonomic axis. It, too, is contraindicated in the first few days of acute myocardial infarction.

4. *Yoga nidra*: This is an advanced relaxative meditation technique which utilizes shavasana, as used by Datey[19], as the basis for deeper and more powerful relaxation. The body is kept motionless and the individual engages in a series of easy mental exercises, such as breath awareness. This is very useful in the acute cardiovascular emergency situation. The technique conserves and redirects energy, taking the focus of our attention away from worries and problems by engaging the mind in neutral and soothing mental activity. It allows the healing process to take place unimpeded by tensions and problems. Breath awareness can be used any time, anywhere. This technique is contraindicated in psychosis, acute anxiety attacks or, rarely, when people dislike the practice, indicating the release of painful, subconscious material into the field of awareness.

A similar regime has recently been reported in the *Journal of the American Medical Association* by Dean Ornish.[20] Ornish conducted a controlled trial over three weeks using stretching techniques, progressive relaxation, breathing techniques, meditation and a low cholesterol diet (no animal products, sugar, salt, alcohol, coffee, processed food). He significantly lowered blood cholesterol and triglycerides in 24 patients. There was also a 90% decline in angina episodes despite increased exercise. Ornish felt that his results were largely due to the patients' change of attitude during the stress management program.[21] He taught his patients to experience less stress and an increased sense of well-being in order to replace the competitive, overachieving 'Type A' behaviour that constantly seeks externally to fulfil an inner sense of lack, and which is thought by many people to be the essential cause of heart disease.

We also prescribe a vegetarian, low fat, low salt diet for heart disease and many other forms of psychosomatic disease, having found that this is an important factor in symptomatic relief and improvement.

Zamarra and his associates also showed an increase in exercise tolerance, maximum work load and delay in onset of ST segment depression in ten angina patients who practised only meditation, compared with controls.[22]

The role of yoga in heart disease

There are two areas where yoga exerts its effects – prevention and cure. On the preventative side yoga deals with:

*   mental tension
*   obesity
*   smoking
*   fatty diet
*   lack of exercise

Yoga is well-known for its ability to reduce weight and relax the autonomic nervous system. Therefore, it can effectively combat two of the major causative factors in heart disease, obesity and mental tension. It also deals with the cravings for cigarettes and fatty foods, which are very much tension related, and implicated in heart problems. Yoga also provides a scientific and systematic series of exercises for physical health which range from dynamic, physically demanding exercises to static and relaxing postures, thereby compensating for a sedentary lifestyle.

In the area of treatment, yoga and meditation are well-known as antidotes for hypertension. Many studies have been done and we do not have to repeat these here as I am sure we are all aware of them. It might be interesting to note that the average blood pressure in the ashram in Munger is 110/70 mm.Hg., despite a busy, active demanding lifestyle which sometimes requires up to eighteen hours of work per day.

It is interesting to note that while yoga has been thought of as being only applicable to essential hypertension we are at present following up a young eight year old boy, diagnosed as having artery stenosis and hypertension. This boy failed to respond to medical therapy, his blood pressure staying persistently at above 140/90 mm.Hg. After commencing yoga, the blood pressure returned to normal levels despite medicine being discontinued.

There are three major areas in heart disease where we have seen yoga work exceedingly well:

1. Coronary artery disease: yoga can be applied to angina, ischaemia and the acute and post-myocardial infarction situation. However, it is to be introduced gradually and progressively under supervision.
2. Arrhythmia.
3. Rheumatic heart disease and coronary bypass surgery.

Coronary artery disease

Angina pectoris: Yoga is of benefit in both the acute situation to reduce pain, and in the chronic situation to reduce the frequency and intensity of the attacks.

In cases of simple angina, yoga can be used to help reduce pain. We occasionally see people in our ashram developing angina because the ashram is located on a large hill and this is a major physical stress. However, they use yoga to remedy this situation. Friedell reported the same thing.[23] Once simple breath awareness has been developed in yoga nidra, it can be translated into the angina situation and often gives as good relief as sublingual medication. The yogic technique is cheaper and has no known side effects. If necessary, drugs can be utilized if yoga does not work fully.

Yogic breath awareness has the added advantage that the patient who masters this technique begins to feel a sense of self-confidence that he or she can master their situation without having to rely on some outside assistance. This increased independence is extremely valuable to heart patients and allows them to develop a better self-image which will aid the process of healing and recovery. It is much better than the defeated, anxiety-provoking image of themselves as 'cardiac cripples'.

In this situation the doctor gains too, as he does not have to deal with the 'neurotic' side of cardiac disease. There is nothing worse than the situation of an unhappy, nagging patient who frequently reappears in the surgery or clinic seeking support and comfort and is prescribed sedative hypnotics instead. Yoga can repair and improve the physical and mental state while the doctor concentrates on treating the disease.

Infarction: It is to be hoped that yoga will prevent ischaemia or infarction from occurring, and controlled trials will be required to find out if this occurs or not.

If ischaemia or infarction do occur then this situation requires that we combine medication with meditation. Physical exercises are strictly forbidden in this situation and only mental exercises are allowed. Indeed, such mental exercises should be encouraged. The technique of yoga nidra and simple breath awareness can be utilized in the intensive care unit.

We have all seen young, seemingly healthy patients who are struck down 'out of the blue' by an unexpected heart attack. They seem to have been previously healthy and pain free; however, often they have been hardworking, have had no holidays, and sacrifice many things, including time with their family, to 'get ahead'. In the hospital they go through the process of denial and then adjustment to their new situation in terms of work, financial security, supporting a family and so on.

These patients also have nothing to do in hospital as they are confined to bed rest with minimal physical activity and, as such, spend much time worrying and feeling anxious, despite tranquillizers and morphine. This turns on their sympathetic activity, and we have seen this sort of situation precipitate a repeated infarction, even within the coronary care unit itself. Worry, anxiety, fear of another attack, insecurity for the future, in themselves, can cause a myocardial infarction. Coronary and intensive care units do not cater for the psychological needs of patients. Drugs are not enough.

The same applies to patients who have had angina, ischaemia or infarction preceding their present attack. They are also subject to the worries, tensions and overactivity of the sympathetic nervous system that the ongoing stress of their situation engenders. They too benefit from yoga nidra in the acute situation.

When coronary artery disease patients begin to recover, yogic exercises are valuable in giving a systematic and gentle series of techniques with which to aid recovery. For example, toe and ankle movements are gentle, relaxing exercises which require no effort but aid circulation especially when combined with breath and awareness. Pawanmuktasana is a series of such easy and simple movements which involve all the body joints and give excellent relaxation when taught properly. It enhances cardiovascular circulation without strain or tension. Certain exercises can even be commenced within the hospital itself.

There are an almost unlimited number of yogic techniques which can be used to relax, energize and strengthen not only the cardiorespiratory system, but the whole body and mind.

Arrhythmia

We have seen yoga work extremely well in certain forms of arrhythmia, in receptive patients. This is especially true for milder forms and earlier cases. However, we have found no reliable parameters by which to judge which patients will benefit. Yoga can be applied to all forms of arrhythmia, no matter what the cause, and can be combined with drug therapy. As the combined regime begins to work, drugs can be reduced and yogic techniques increased.

Yoga and surgery

Yoga has been successfully used to avoid coronary bypass surgery and to maintain the heart in good working condition where costs of the operation were prohibitive. Rheumatic heart disease is very common in India and we see many cases of young people either unable to afford the extreme costs of surgery or who were so frightened by the prospect of surgery that they could not face it.

The anxiety engendered by the thought of surgery increases sympathetic nervous activity, heart rate, blood pressure and so on, and precipitates rapid degeneration of cardiac status, requiring increased dosages of all medication. Drugs cannot successfully allay this anxiety unless such high doses are given that they wipe out the individual's normal conscious state and increase the side effects beyond the limits of endurance. A few simple yogic techniques by themselves or in concert with a mild drug regime is often sufficient to allay anxiety and induce a relaxed, relatively cheerful state. By slowing decompensation, patients who cannot afford surgery can live a better, more active life, for a longer period of time.

In cases where surgery is required and consent is given, we have found that yoga, preoperatively practised from two to six months is valuable in maintaining cardiac stability. We also hypothesize that after surgery, yoga may help to reduce or eliminate further degeneration and thereby prevent recurrence, as well as providing gentle, progressive exercises for the cardiorespiratory system. As well as this it may prevent complications such as deep venous thrombosis.

Once again, certain techniques can be used in the hospital situation both to reduce pain and speed recovery. Several studies have highlighted yoga's ability to reduce pain, especially the psychological component.[24,25] Yogis are famous for their ability to endure pain and austerity and it will be interesting to investigate yoga's ability to affect the nervous system, endorphines and other physiological factors involved in pain, especially related to heart disease.

Case history 1

A senior major in the Australian Staff Corps sustained two myocardial infarctions between May and June 1972. Between 1972–74 he sustained three more infarcts. He was told that he would have to be confined to limited physical activity and was put onto nineteen different medications.

Against all advice, he came to Munger to the Bihar School of Yoga in 1974 and practised pawanmuktasana, simple pranayama and yoga nidra plus a few meditative practices. Today he is off all medication, having stopped his Inderal in 1980. Leading an active life, he commenced university studies in 1976, graduating with a Masters of Behavioural Science in 1980 and living as a private psychologist, director of a community centre and hospital clinical psychologist. He also travels regularly.

He revisited Munger in 1983 and reported that he was pain-free and able to function at a normal level, but that regular blood pressure checks and a regulated lifestyle were necessary so that both stress and fat do not accumulate. He stated, "My life is full, joyous and boundless."

Case history 2
One case in which yoga helped to avoid coronary bypass surgery is that of a colonel in the Indian Army, aged 56 years, who approached us in June 1982 stating that he was a candidate for coronary bypass surgery due to intractable angina, but could yoga do anything for him? He was suffering from severe angina which was brought on by walking even on the flat ground for a few minutes as well as by emotional stress. He commenced simple yoga practices and in late 1983 reported feeling so well that he stopped all medication, under his physician's guidance, and has recently completed a four-month tour around India, from Gangotri to Madurai.

This man is presently actively engaged in his work and feels as though he has been given a new lease on life. He still experiences mild angina from time to time; however, it is relieved by taking rest. We intend to follow up on his coronary artery status in the near future to objectify our findings. If walking in the mountains is a good exercise-tolerance test, then this case history exemplifies yoga's capacity to restore relatively normal cardiac function and a normal lifestyle.

Case history 3

A 51 year old gentleman suffered an anteroseptal myocardial infarct in 1980. An ECG in September 1983 showed that there was T wave inversion in V2 and V3 and Q waves in V2. He started yoga in December 1983 and an ECG taken in 1984 was normal, indicating improved cardiac status. He has taken himself off his medication and feels much improved. He will require further follow-up to assess this encouraging initial improvement. He is a typical example of those we see in cases of ischaemic heart disease who start to practise yoga before complications set in.

Respiratory disease

Yoga also has a lot to offer for respiratory diseases. For example, asthma, which the author personally suffered from in the allergic form for 14 years before curing himself through yoga 10 years ago, is easily amenable to yoga in both the acute and chronic situations. It is a very common experience in our ashram to see people come to us wheezing and coughing and suffering from sinusitis and allergy, and after two weeks of yoga and change of diet for them to feel a wonderful subjective improvement. Tandon has also reported that he has found subjective improvement even in severe COAD through the use of yogic techniques.[26]

Conclusion

Yoga is cheap, simple and effective when properly taught and practised. It requires only 20 to 30 minutes in the morning and 10 to 20 minutes at night to achieve a noticeable effect and improved relaxation. Of course, slightly longer practice will give an even better effect, especially in the therapeutic situation. Often practices can be tailored to need. For example, a busy doctor or executive may practise ten minutes before or after food and ten minutes before sleep and achieve an equally good result. In the intensive care ward, two or three sessions of 20 to 30 minutes are required.

124

Both the patient and the doctor will benefit from a close relationship between yoga and medicine. With an increasing number of people being disappointed by medical treatment and turning to other lines of therapy, it is well worth our while to do good experimental trials to both convince ourselves and to inform the public of which methods are useful and effective. Yoga stands ready to back up its claims, and until some more effective form of treatment is devised, the medical community should look further into this side of healing.

As doctors, we should put ourselves in our patient's position and ask ourselves, if we had heart disease, which treatment we would prefer – medicine, surgery or yoga? Common sense points to yoga.

Despite the need for statistical evidence and evaluation of yoga, the concept of total patient care points to the fact that we should be using meditation, relaxation and other proven methods of dealing with the psychological side of psychosomatic disease. In the long run science may further validate yoga as an invaluable aid in the cure of many heart diseases.

Message to Doctors

As doctors you have a major task ahead of you. You are the traditional guides of the community in health matters. People have always looked to you for help, not only in their physical problems but also in their mental, emotional and spiritual ones. These are the roles of the physician and doctor which society has laid before you. You bear an enormous responsibility in shaping community attitudes, ideals and expectations. Your words carry respect in all segments of the community, and this is why it is vital that you become personally familiar with yoga as a way of life, as well as a cure of disease. You must incorporate it with your other diagnostic, prescribing, healing and educating skills.

Yoga is preventive medicine firstly, and it is curative medicine secondly. More and more of your patients are looking for ways to improve their mental and physical health. They don't want only a tablet for their pains any more. Many want to be shown a scientific way to improve their lives; one which guarantees physical health, mental peace and spiritual enlightenment. They want a realistic solution, a way to cope positively with their mental and emotional problems and difficulties. Tranquillizers, sedatives and sleeping pills are no longer enough.

If this were not the case, why would so many people be looking to swamis from outside their own culture to provide a meaningful way and path in life? Of course, we accept this, because it is our duty as sannyasins to serve and teach those who sincerely seek yoga, but please do not depend on us.

Everyone wants to know the practices, the sadhana for them to overcome their specific physical and mental problems and to hasten their personal evolution as well. So often there are physical problems which have failed to respond to medical or surgical treatment. Then there are so many mental disturbances, like anxiety, neurosis, phobias, fears, emotional suppressions, frustrations and psychosomatic symptoms. Medical science has offered tranquillizers and sedatives, but no real solutions.

Very frequently we find that yoga is able to provide solutions for these problems. In my own experience, I can assure you of this. Yoga is a science which has to be prescribed practically and scientifically just like a medicine. Yoga is a therapeutic science which can be correctly prescribed only after the medical history, examinations, tests and x-rays have been performed and the diagnosis is known. Yoga will cure sinusitis, eosinophilia, allergy, asthma, tonsillitis, ulcer, indigestion, migraine, headache, angina, colitis, arthritis, skin diseases. The list is endless, but yoga therapy is certainly not brought about by waving a magic wand; it is first and foremost a science. It requires a thorough knowledge of anatomy, physiology and psychology if it is to be practised for therapeutic purposes. Who then is more qualified than doctors to prescribe and utilize yoga?

But first you must experience yoga for yourselves, and once you know and practise it, then you can begin to teach and prescribe it on the basis of your personal experiences. You must not accept yoga on the basis of faith alone. Even if you want to do so, I do not accept it. You are scientists, highly trained in logic and experimental analysis. You must conduct your own experiments – first with yourselves and then with the help of your patients. You must submit yoga to a deep and thorough scrutiny, and only then accept it if you wish. Yoga is not a pseudoscience. Yoga is definitely a science, just as pharmacology, physiology and pathology are sciences.

Start your own clinical trials. Use yoga either alone or in conjunction with your other therapies. You must run comparisons and control trials. Prescribe neti for sinusitis and see if those patients are better off after one month in comparison to those who take anti-histamines instead; prescribe yoga nidra for your coronary angina patients and reassess their clinical state after six weeks compared to those who use a glyceryl trinitrate under the tongue when coronary pain arises. Observe your results and draw your own conclusions. Then, when your numbers are sufficient, publish your results in the journals. In this way only will yoga emerge for what it is, a pure science, which stands up to clinical trial and evaluation. If the healing potential of the yoga techniques is to become known to suffering mankind, then it must become a part of medical therapeutics. You must perform the clinical trials and evaluations which will validate yoga. This is the next step.

References

Introduction to Heart Disease
[1]Stern, M.P. 1979, *Annals of Internal Medicine*, Nov. 1979.

Q.2 Hypertension
[1]Benson, H., Costa, R., Garcia-Palmieri, M.R. et al., 'Coronary heart disease factors: a comparison of two Puerto Rican populations', *American Journal of Public Health*, 56, 1966, pp. 1057–1060.

[2]Berkson, D.M., Stamber, J., Lindberg, H.A. et al., 'Socio-economic correlates of athero-sclerotic and hypertensive heart disease', *Annals of New York Academy of Science*, 84, 1960, pp. 835–850.

[3]Russek, H.L. and Zohman, B.L., 'Relative significance of heredity, diet and occupational stress in coronary heart disease in young adults', *American Journal of Medical Sciences*, 235, 1958, pp. 266–275.

[4]Datey, K.K. and Bhagat, S.J., 'Stress and heart disease and how to control it with biofeedback and shavasana', *Quarterly Journal of Surgical Sciences*, 13(3,4), Sept–Dec. 1977.

[5]Brauer, P., Horlick, L., Nelson, E., Farquhar, J.W. and Agras, W.S., 'Relaxation therapy for essential hypertension: a Veteran's Administration outpatients study', *Journal of Behavioural Medicine*, 1979.

[6]Patel, C., 'Yoga and biofeedback in the management of hypertension', *Lancet*, Nov. 10. 1973.

Q.3 Essential Hypertension and its Complications
[1]Patel, C., 'Coronary risk factor reduction through biofeedback-aided relaxation and meditation', *Journal of the Royal College of General Practitioners*, 27, 1977, pp. 401–405.

[2]Rosenman, R.H., 'The role of behavior patterns and neurogenic factors in the pathogenesis of coronary heart disease', in R.S. Eliot (Ed.), *Stress and the Heart*, Futura, N.Y., 1974, pp. 123–141.

[3]Cooper, M.J. and Aygen, M.M., 'A relaxation technique in the management of hypercholesterolemia', *Journal of Human Stress*, 5, 1979, pp. 24–27.

[4]Udupa, K.N., Singh, R.H. and Settiwar, R.M., 'A comparative study on the effect of some individual yogic practices in normal persons', *Indian Journal of Medical Research*, 63, 1975, p. 1066–1071.

[5]Harris, J., 'Relaxation training as a stress-reducing technique for persons with diabetes', *Dissertations Abstracts International*, 41(9), 1981, pp. 3573–3574.

[6]Melkote, Varandani, Rukmini and Sinha, 'Diabetes and yoga', *Proceedings of 1st and 2nd Scientific Seminars of the Central Council for Research in Indian Medicine*, 1973 and 1975.

[7]Lavgankar, P.L. et al., *Report of Yogopchar Shibir*, Yoga Vidya Dham, Poona, 1974.

[8]Panda, N.C., 'Report of the diabetes camp at Bihar School of Yoga, Calcutta Unit, 1976', *Yoga*, 17(2), Feb. 1979.

[9]Mishra, S.K., 'Diabetes mellitis and its management by yoga in diabetes and obesity', in J. Vague and P. Vague (Eds.), *Int. Cong. Series No. 454*, Excerpta Medica, Amsterdam, 1979, pp. 373–379.

Q.4 Heart Disease

[1]Rosenman, R.H., in R.S. Eliot (Ed.), *Stress and the Heart*, op. cit.

[2]'Androgens: to the heart of the matter', *Science*, Feb. 15, 1980.

[3]Masseri, A., L'Abbate, A., Baraldi, G. et al., 'Coronary vasospasm as a possible cause of myocardial infarction: a conclusion derived from a study of preinfarction angina', *New England Journal of Medicine*, 299, 1978, pp. 1271–1277.

[4]Orme-Johnson, D.W., 'Autonomic stability and transcendental meditation', *Psychosomatic Medicine*, 35(4), July–Aug., 1973, pp. 341–349.

[5]Puente, A. and Berman, I., 'The effects of behaviour therapy, self-relaxation and transcendental meditation on cardiovascular stress response', *Journal of Clinical Psychology*, 36, pp. 291–293.

[6]Lakshmikanthan, C., 'Long term effects of yoga on hypertension and for coronary artery disease', *Journal of Association of Physicians of India*, 12, Dec. 27, 1979, pp. 1055–1058.

[7]Motoyama, H., 'Yoga and oriental medicine', *Journal of International Association for Religion and Parapsychology*, Tokyo, 5(1), 1979.

Q.5 Cardiac Arrhythmias

[1]Motoyama, H., 'Western and eastern medical studies of pranayama and heart control', *Journal of International Association for Religion and Parapsychology*, Tokyo 3(1), June 1977.

[2]Brosse, T., 'Etudes instrumentales des techniques du yoga' (Investigations using scientific instruments of the effects of yoga practices), *Publications de l'Ecole Francaise d'Extreme Orient*, L11, Paris, 1976.

[3]Anand, B. and Chinna, G., 'Investigations on yogis claiming to stop their heartbeats', *Indian Journal of Medical Research*, 49, 1961, pp. 90–94.

[4]Von Hildebrandt, G., 'The co-ordination of rhythmic functions in humans', *Proceedings German Society of Internal Medicine, 73rd Congress*, 1967, pp. 921–941.

[5]Friedell, A., 'Automatic attentive breathing in angina pectoris', *Minnesota Medicine*, Aug., 1948, pp. 875–881.

Q.6 Stroke

[1]'Application of Yoga in Rehabilitational Therapy', Report. 1st Congress Czech and Slovak Commissions for Use of Yoga in Rehabilitation, Kosice, 1978.

Q.7 Cerebral Degeneration

[1]Hunziker, O., Abdel'Al, S. and Schulz, U., *Journal of Gerontology*, 3, 1979, pp. 345.

[2]Rao, S., 'Metabolic cost of headstand posture', *Journal of Applied Physiology*, 17(1), 1962, pp. 117–118

[3]Gaertner, H. et al., 'Influence of sirshasana', paper delivered at 10th Congress International Haematology Society, Stockholm, 1964.

[4]Jevning, R., Wilson, A.F., Smith, W.R. and Morton, M.E., 'Redistribution of blood flow in acute hypometabolic behaviour', *American Journal of Physiology*, 235 (1), 1978, pp. 89–92.

[5]Motoyama, H., 'An electrophysiological study of prana (ki)', *Journal of International Association for Religion and Parapsychology*, 4(1), 1978.

Q.8 Peripheral Vascular Disease

[1]Gopal, K.S., Anantharaman, V., Nishith, S.D. and Bhatnagar, O.P., 'The effect of yogasanas on muscular tone and cardiorespiratory adjustments', *Indian Journal of Medical Sciences*, 28(10), 1974, pp. 438–443.

[2]Jevning, R. et al., op. cit.

[3]Chohan, I.S., Nayar, H.S., Thomas, P. and Greetha, N.S., 'Influence of yoga on blood coagulation', *Journal of Associations or Physicians of India*, 27(9), Sept. 1979.

Q.9 Raynaud's Disease

[1]Gopal, K.S. et al., op. cit.

[2]Bhatnagar, O.P. and Anantharaman, V., 'The effect of yoga training on neuromuscular excitability and muscular relaxation', *Neurology India*, 25(4), Dec., 1977, pp. 230–232.

[3]West, M.A., 'Physiological effects of meditation: longitudinal study', *British Journal of Clinical Psychology*, 18(2), 1979, pp. 219–226.

[4]Orme-Johnson, D.W., op. cit.

[5]Agrawal, R.C. et al., 'Effects of shavasana on vascular response to a cold pressor test in hyperreactors', *Indian Heart Journal*, 29(4), 1977, pp. 182–185.

[6]Bhatnagar, O.P., Kanguly, A.K. and Anantharaman, V., 'Influence of yoga training on thermoregulation', *Indian Journal of Medical Research*, 67, May, 1978, pp. 844–847.

[7]Werbach, M.L. et al., 'Peripheral temperatures of migraineurs undergoing relaxation training', *Headache*, 18(4), 1978, pp. 211–214.

[8]Rama, Swami, *Voluntary Control Project*, Menninger Foundation, Kansas, USA.

[9]Surwit, S., Pilon, N. and Fenton, H.C., 'Behavioral treatment of Raynaud's disease', *Journal of Behavioral Medicine*, 1(3), 1978, pp. 323–325.

Q.10 Arteriosclerotic Degenerative Diseases

[1]Udupa, K.N., 'A manual of science and philosophy of yoga', *Journal of Research in Indian Medicine, Yoga and Homeopathy*, 2(1), 1976, pp. 49–54.

[2]Satyananda Saraswati, Swami, 'Siddhasana and the heart', *Yoga*, 19(3), March 1981, pp. 29–32.

Q.11 Respiratory Diseases

[1]Gupta, G.B., Sepaha, G.C., Menou, I. And Tiwari, S.K., 'The effects of yoga on bronchial asthma', *Yoga*, 17(2), Feb. 1979, pp. 29–33.

[2]Hornsberger, R. and Wilson, A.F., 'The effects of transcendental meditation on bronchial asthma', *Clinical Research*, 21, 1973, pp. 273.

[3]Zeltzer, L., *Report of University of Texas Health Science Center*, 1980.

[4]Tandon, M.K., 'Adjunct treatment with yoga in chronic severe airways obstruction', *Thorax*, 33, 1978, pp. 514–517.

[5]Blokhin, I.P. and Shanmugan, T.M., 'Asanas and breathing', *Sechenov Physiology Journal USSR*, 59(4), 1973, pp. 632–638.

[6]Rao, S., 'Metabolic cost of headstand posture', *Journal of Applied Physiology*, 17(1), 1962, pp. 117–118.

[7]Miles, W.R., 'Oxygen consumption during three yoga type breathing patterns', *Journal of Applied Physiology*, 19(1), 1964, pp. 75–82.

Q.12 Cancer

[1]Meares, A., 'Regression of cancer of the rectum after intensive meditation', *Medical Journal Australia*, 2(10), 1979, pp. 539.

[2]Meares, A., 'Remission of massive metastasis from undifferentiated carcinoma of the lung associated with intensive meditation', *Journal of the American Society of Psychosomatic Dentistry and Medicine*, 27(2), 1980, pp. 40–41.

[3]Meares, A., 'Regression of cancer after intensive meditation, followed by death', *Medical Journal Australia*, 2(11), 1979, pp. 374–375.

[4]Simonton, O.C. and Simonton, S., *Journal of Transpersonal Psychology*, 7, 1975, pp. 29.

[5]Scarf, M., 'Images that heal: a doubtful idea whose time has come', *Psychology Today*, Sept. 1980.

[6]Suzuki, J., Yamauchi, Y., Horikawa, M. and Yamagata, S., 'Fasting therapy for psychosomatic diseases with special reference to its indication and therapeutic mechanism', *Toheku Journal of Experimental Medicine*, 118, 1976, pp. 245–259.

[7]Udupa, K.N., 'A manual of science and philosophy of yoga', *Journal of Research in Indian Medicine, Yoga and Homeopathy,* 2(1), 1976, pp. 58–59.

Yogic Methods in Cardiopulmonary Diseases

[1]Datey, K.K. et al., 'Shavasana, a Yogic Exercise in the Management of Hypertension', *Angiology,* 20, 1969, pp. 325–333.

[2]Erskine-Willis, J. et al., 'Relaxation Therapy in Asthma – a critical review', *Psychosomatic Medicine* (USA), 43(4), pp. 81.

[3]Friedell, A., 'Automatic Attentive Breathing in Angina Pectoris', *Minnesota Medicine*, Aug. 1948.

[4]Harris, Joan Ann, 'Relaxation Training as a Stress-Reducing Technique for Persons with Diabetes', *Dissertations Abstracts International*, 41(9), 1981, pp. 3573–81.

[5]Susen, G.R., 'Conditional Relaxation in a Case of Ulcerative Colitis', *Journal of Behavioral Therapy & Experimental Psychiatry*, 9, pp. 283.

[6]Patel, C., 'Yoga & Biofeedback in Management of Hypertension', *The Lancet*, Nov. 10, 1973.

[7]Tandon, M.K., 'Adjunct Treatment with Yoga in Chronic Severe Airways Obstruction', *Thorax,* 33, 1978, pp. 514–7.

[8]West, M.A., 'Meditation and the EEG', *Psychological Medicine*, 10, 1980, pp. 369–75.

[9]Wallace, R.K. & Benson, H., 'The Physiology of Meditation', *Scientific America,* Feb. 226(2), 1972, pp. 84–90.

[10]Banquet, J.P., 'Spectral Analysis of EEG in Meditation', *EEG & Clinical Neurophysiology,* Aug. 35(2), 1973, pp. 143–51.

[11]Michaels, R.R. et al., 'Renin Corticol & Aldosterone during TM', *Experiencia,* 34, 1978, pp. 618–9.

[12]Udupa, et al., 'Studies on Physiological, Endocrine and Metabolic Response to the Practice of Yoga', *Journal of Research of Indian Medicine*, VI(3), 1971.

[13]Kabat-Zinn, J., 'An Outpatient Program in Behavioural Medicine for Chronic pain Patients Based on the practice of Mindfulness Meditation. Theoretical Considerations and preliminary Results', *General Hospital Psychiatry*, 4, 1982, pp. 33–47.

[14]Mills, W.W. & Farrow, J.T., 'The T.M. Technique and Acute Experimental Pain', *Psychosomatic Medicine*, April, 43(2), 1981, pp. 157–64.

[15]Anderson, A., 'How the Mind Heals', *Psychology Today*, Dec. 1982.

[16]'Breathing Cycle linked to Hemispheric Dominance', *Brain Mind Bulletin*, 8(3), Jan., 1983.

[17]Ibid.

[18]Ibid.

[19]Datey, op. cit.

[20]Ornish D., *Journal of the American Medical Association*, 249, 1983, pp. 54–59.

[21]'Stress/diet programs strengthens diseased heart', *Brain Mind Bulletin*, Jan. 24, 8(4). 1983.

[22]Zamarra, J.W. et al., 'The effects of the TM program on the Exercise Performance of patients with Angina Pectoris', *Scientific Research on TM, Selected Papers*, Vol.I. paper 35, pp. 270–78.

[23]Friedell, op. cit.

[24]Kabat-Zinn, op. cit.

[25]Mills, W.W. & Farrow, J.T., op. cit.

[26]Tandon, op. cit.

INTERNATIONAL YOGA FELLOWSHIP MOVEMENT (IYFM)

The IYFM is a charitable and philosophical movement founded by Swami Satyananda at Rajnandgaon in 1956 to disseminate the yogic tradition throughout the world. It forms the medium to convey the teachings of Swami Satyananda through its affiliated centres around the world. Swami Niranjanananda is the first Paramacharya of the International Yoga Fellowship Movement.

The IYFM provides guidance, systematized yoga training programs and sets teaching standards for all the affiliated yoga teachers, centres and ashrams. A Yoga Charter to consolidate and unify the humanitarian efforts of all sannyasin disciples, yoga teachers, spiritual seekers and well-wishers was introduced during the World Yoga Convention in 1993. Affiliation to this Yoga Charter enables the person to become a messenger of goodwill and peace in the world, through active involvement in various far-reaching yoga-related projects.

BIHAR SCHOOL OF YOGA (BSY)

The Bihar School of Yoga is a charitable and educational institution founded by Swami Satyananda at Munger in 1963, with the aim of imparting yogic training to all nationalities and to provide a focal point for a mass return to the ancient science of yoga. The Chief Patron of Bihar School of Yoga is Swami Niranjanananda. The original school, Sivanandashram, is the centre for the Munger locality. Ganga Darshan, the new school established in 1981, is situated on a historic hill with panoramic views of the river Ganges.

Yoga Health Management, Teacher Training, Sadhana, Kriya Yoga and other specialized courses are held throughout the year. BSY is also renowned for its sannyasa training and the initiation of female and foreign sannyasins.

BSY provides trained sannyasins and teachers for conducting yoga conventions, seminars and lectures tours around the world. It also contains a comprehensive research library and scientific research centre.

SIVANANDA MATH (SM)

Sivananda Math is a social and charitable institution founded by Swami Satyananda at Munger in 1984, in memory of his guru, Swami Sivananda Saraswati of Rishikesh. The Head Office is now situated at Rikhia in Deoghar district, Bihar. Swami Niranjanananda is the Chief Patron.

Sivananda Math aims to facilitate the growth of the weaker and underprivileged sections of society, especially rural communities. Its activities include: distribution of free scholarships, clothing, farm animals and food, the digging of tube-wells and construction of houses for the needy, assistance to farmers in ploughing and watering their fields. The Rikhia complex also houses a satellite dish system for providing global information to the villagers.

A medical clinic has been established for the provision of medical treatment, advice and education. Veterinary services are also provided. All services are provided free and universally to everyone, regardless of caste and creed.

YOGA RESEARCH FOUNDATION (YRF)

The Yoga Research Foundation is a scientific, research-oriented institution founded by Swami Satyananda at Munger in 1984. Swami Niranjanananda is the Chief Patron of the foundation.

YRF aims to provide an accurate assessment of the practices of different branches of yoga within a scientific framework, and to establish yoga as an essential science for the development of mankind. At present the foundation is working on projects in the areas of fundamental research and clinical research. It is also studying the effects of yoga on proficiency improvement in various social projects, e.g. army, prisoners, children. These projects are being carried out at affiliated centres worldwide.

YRF's future plans include literary, scriptural, medical and scientific investigations into other little-known aspects of yoga for physical health, mental well-being and spiritual upliftment.

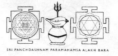

SRI PANCHDASHNAM PARAMAHAMSA ALAKH BARA

SRI PANCHDASHNAM PARAMAHAMSA
ALAKH BARA (PPAB)

Sri Panchdashnam Paramahamsa Alakh Bara was established in 1990 by Swami Satyananda at Rikhia, Deoghar, Bihar. It is a charitable educational and non-profit making institution aiming to uphold and propagate the highest tradition of sannyasa, namely vairagya (dis passion), tyaga (renunciation) and tapasya (austerity). It propound: the tapovan style of living adopted by the rishis and munis of the vedic era and is intended only for sannyasins, renunciates, ascetics tapasvis and paramahamsas. The Alakh Bara does not conduct an activities such as yoga teaching or preaching of any religion o religious concepts. The guidelines set down for the Alakh Bara are based on the classical vedic tradition of sadhana, tapasya an swadhyaya, or atma chintan.

Swami Satyananda, who resides permanently at the Alakh Bara has performed the Panchagni Vidya and other vedic sadhanas, thu paving the way for future paramahamsas to uphold their tradition.

बिहार योग भारती
BIHAR YOGA BHARATI

BIHAR YOGA BHARATI (BYB)

Bihar Yoga Bharati was founded by Swami Niranjanananda in 199 as an educational and charitable institution for advanced studies i yogic sciences. It is the culmination of the vision of Swami Sivanand and Swami Satyananda. BYB is the world's first government accrec ted university wholly devoted to teaching yoga. A comprehensiv yogic education is imparted with provision to grant higher degree in yogic studies such as MA, MSc, MPhil, DLitt, and PhD to the st dents. It offers a complete scientific and yogic education accordir to the needs of today, through the faculties of Yoga Philosoph Yoga Psychology, Applied Yogic Science and Yogic Ecology.

Residential courses of four months to two years are conducted a gurukul environment, so that along with yoga education, the spi of seva (selfless service), samarpan (dedication) and karuna (comp? sion) for humankind is also imbibed by the students.

YOGA PUBLICATIONS TRUST (YPT)